TheOpen
University

KU-489-100

Arts: A second-level course
Understanding Music: Elements, Techniques and Styles

UNIT 14

FOLLOWING A SCORE II

UNIT 15

TWO-STAVE REDUCTION

UNIT 16

MOSTLY REVISION

The Open University

The Open University, Walton Hall, Milton Keynes MK7 6AA

First published 1994. Reprinted 1998

Edited, designed and typeset by the Open University.

Printed in Great Britain by Selwood Printing Ltd. Burgess Hill, West Sussex.

ISBN 0 7492 1121 0

This text forms part of an Open University Second-Level Course. If you would like a copy of *Studying with the Open University*, please write to the Central Enquiry Service, PO Box 200, The Open University, Walton Hall, Milton Keynes, MK7 6YZ. If you have not already enrolled on the Course and would like to buy this or other Open University material, please write to Open University Educational Enterprises Ltd, 12 Cofferidge Close, Stony Stratford, Milton Keynes MK11 1BY, United Kingdom.

1.2

7541C/a214u14i1.2

UNIT 14

FOLLOWING A SCORE II

Prepared for the Course Team by J. Barrie Jones

CONTENTS

DAY 1	1
	2-2.1
	2.2-2.3
DAY 2	3-3.2
	3.3
	3.4
	4
DAY 3	5-5.1
	5.2-5.4
DAY 4	6-6.2
	6.3-6.5

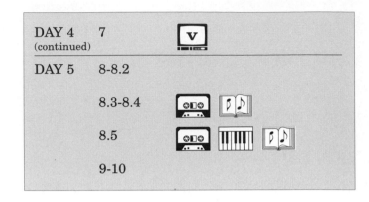

Audio items for this unit can be found on Audio-cassette 6.

Video items are on Video-cassette 2.

You will need Scores 2 and your scores of Beethoven's Fifth Symphony and Tchaikovsky's *Serenade for Strings*.

1 CONTENT AND AIMS

The preceding three units extended your harmonic vocabulary and introduced you both to the concept of modulation and to the way in which it works in practice. There has been a fair amount of material both to learn and to assimilate. In some respects Units 14 and 15 return to and build upon the reading skills that you acquired in Unit 9. There is thus not much new material that has to be 'learnt' in Unit 14, although you should try to remember the historical background material that I introduce. You should find, though, that conscientiously working through the exercises keeps you fully occupied for the week. It is important that you do these exercises carefully. If, by any chance, you have time to spare at the end of the week, go through the more difficult ones again: regular practice in score reading is the only sure way to fluency.

As I have suggested, Unit 14 is complementary to Unit 9. That is to say, the score-reading skills of this unit consist of exercises in following varying types of score. In some scores I have marked appropriate places (or I will get you to highlight them) so as to help you find and keep your bearings.

The unit has two main aims, and they are quite straightforward. My first aim is to introduce you to the format of scores with more staves than you encountered in Unit 9. The musical textures will be more complex than those you met in Unit 9, and will be drawn from a wider repertoire: keyboard, chamber and orchestral music. The second aim is to consider in some detail two new clefs, the alto and tenor clefs, which were briefly touched upon earlier in the course. The alto is the standard clef for the viola; the tenor is found in high cello and bassoon parts, and is the usual clef for the tenor trombone, though not, fortunately perhaps, for tenors in choirs! By the end of the unit you should be able to follow scores of up to five staves without too much difficulty, and be able to 'scan' a score so that the salient points are recognized by your ear and eye and then retained, in part at least, by the brain. These landmarks in a score are useful on two counts: they prevent your getting lost, and they often give useful clues to the structure of the music you are studying. In the unit you will practise reading (or scanning) vertically as well as horizontally, and with luck take in up to three or four different clefs all at once. No mean achievement!

There are two video sections, and these divide the unit into three blocks. You will need a pencil and music manuscript paper for both video sections. Television Programme 4 is associated with this unit, and it would be useful for you to have reached as far as, and including, the second video section by the time the programme is transmitted, if at all possible.

Some of the shorter extracts of score are printed here in the unit. The remaining extracts appear in Scores 2. You will also need your scores of the Tchaikovsky *Serenade for Strings* and Beethoven's Fifth Symphony.

The extracts are recorded on Audio-cassette 6. You will find it helpful to provide your own counter-readings for each item, since you may want to select individual items yourself for further replayings. In any case, I shall use a number of items again in Unit 15.

As in Unit 9, you will not need your keyboard, except for a couple of optional exercises. Throughout the unit, you will find that a highlighting pen will be useful.

2 PIANO SCORES

2.1 BEETHOVEN: 'WALDSTEIN' SONATA
CHOPIN: PRELUDE IN C MINOR

At this stage in the course, you may feel that it is a little elementary to return to two-stave-reading in the form of piano music. However, some piano textures are difficult to follow, since keyboard figurations can be tricky to take in at a first hearing. Don't feel too affronted yet! I want to go back briefly to two short extracts from Unit 9, in order that we can proceed – in the words of Sherlock Holmes – from the known to the unknown. Look back at Examples 4(b) and 4(a) in Section 3 of Unit 9. These are played as Items 1 and 2 on Audio-cassette 6, associated with this unit, and printed below as Examples 1 and 2. Listen to these now as a revision exercise, but if you feel confident about reading piano scores, proceed to Section 2.2. If, however, you are unsure, or if you get lost, read the remainder of this sub-section very carefully – then try again.

 LISTEN TO ITEMS 1 AND 2 WHILE FOLLOWING EXAMPLES 1 AND 2.

Example 1   Beethoven: Sonata in C, Op. 53, 'Waldstein'

Example 2   Chopin: Prelude in C minor Op. 28 No 20

I hope that you are reasonably sure of what to look for as you follow these scores. The extract from the 'Waldstein' Sonata is from the end of the development section in the first movement, and Beethoven exploits what had been until very recently the highest note available to him on his piano – the F – by gradually leading up to it, then fashioning a repeated motive that continually returns to that note. I have marked this F in the score with crosses. The repeated low G in the left hand (the first six of which I have marked with circles) is almost the *lowest* note on Beethoven's piano. So the music has a widely spaced, two-part texture which, coupled with the busyness of the semiquavers, help to create a feeling of excitement. No doubt you can hear this without recourse to the score, but your enjoyment of the music is, I hope, enhanced by your being able to examine and follow the score.

If following it still seems difficult, *listen* to the music without the score, counting aloud the four beats to each bar. Then listen to and follow the score, matching what you have done in your head with the signposts in the notation: high Fs, low Gs, and so on. It if helps, use your highlighting pen to mark perhaps the first and third beats of each bar. Keep persevering!

The stately chorale-like tread of Chopin's C minor Prelude (Example 2) is obviously very different from the Beethoven. And the way in which you read the score is different too. The slow tempo ensures that every chord can be followed as it is played, without too much difficulty.[1] However, in neither piece do you read every single note, any more than you read every single alphabetical letter in a piece of prose. The Chopin example contains too many notes per chord, while the rapidity of individual notes in the 'Waldstein' would make such reading impossible. As I suggested, most musicians would 'read' the Beethoven by being aware of the underlying pulse (four or even two beats to each bar) and following the gradual ascent of the melody to the high F in the right hand. Perhaps twice a bar, then, there's a point where you can be reasonably sure of where you are. If you also know what is happening in the texture, then you can follow the score without attempting to read each note. You can appreciate, therefore, that successful score reading combines a knowledge of tempo, textures, dynamics – and common sense. The first three will all vary from one work to the next, and frequently within the same work. Each fresh piece of music that you meet will need to be assessed in this way. The remainder of this unit will attempt to provide some helpful hints for doing this.

2.2   CHOPIN: PRELUDE IN C MAJOR

The next example is another Chopin Prelude from the same set of twenty-four as Example 2, Op. 28 (1836–9). This is No. 1, in C major, recorded as Item 3 on the audio-cassette. The score is given in Scores 2 (p. 25). Listen to the music, following the score, and then list the points of reference in the music which enable you to keep up with it. Your list might be different from mine, though what you have written may well be equally valid.

 LISTEN TO ITEM 3 WHILE FOLOWING THE SCORE (SCORES 2, p. 25).

Figure 1   Frédéric Chopin (1810–1849). Drawing by Eugène Delacroix, 1838. (Musée du Louvre).

---

[1]   Incidentally, bar 3 has posed an interesting musicological problem, as the last chord has E♭ in some editions and E♮ in others. There are a number of sources for the Preludes, not all of which agree on this point. Even Chopin's 'final version' – if it were known – might be unavailing since he may merely have omitted to supply an accidental he actually intended. Our recording and score has an E♭, but you often hear E♮.

Here is my list.

1 The first bass note of each bar. This assists in propelling the music forward in addition to supporting the melody and harmony.

2 The *crescendo* and *stretto* half-way through the piece, culminating in a sudden *piano* at bar 25. (*Stretto* in this context is equivalent to *accelerando*: gradually getting faster. The word *stretto* has a quite different meaning in fugue, both of which you will study in Unit 30.)

3 The octave leap G–G in the left-hand between the first note of bars 7 and 8.

4 The repeated Cs in the bass during the last ten bars.

Mark these points in your score if you find it helpful. If you still find it hard following the score, try counting 'one in a bar' to start with.

You may have wondered about two other small points: the Gothic-style 'Ped' markings and the asterisks. These are quite common in some editions. The pianist depresses the right (or sustaining) pedal at Ped (which need not necessarily be printed in Gothic type) and lifts the pedal at the *. All the notes played are then sustained because the dampers have been separated from the strings. Notice, in bars 1–4 and towards the end, the occasional left-hand note with a long stem extending upwards into the right-hand stave. This, too, is quite frequent in Romantic piano music and indicates that such notes, though in the lower stave, are played by the right hand. It can save leger lines, contributes to the visual clarity of the notation on the page, and separates the parts visually.

2.3 BRAHMS: INTERMEZZO IN C MAJOR

Now turn to the extract from Brahms's Intermezzo in C, Op. 119 No. 3, in Scores 2 (p. 24). It was composed in 1892.

Bars 1–24 are the first section of a ternary scheme. Before you listen to the music, look at the extract (always a sensible thing to do in any case). Notice the time signature. (You could try tapping out a couple of bars of $\frac{6}{8}$ quavers). Look at the tempo marking: *Grazioso e giocoso*, here an indication of mood, 'gracefully and joyfully'. Notice the register used, as well as the texture, so that you have an inkling of what to expect. Now listen to the music several times while following the score, then answer the questions in the following exercise.

LISTEN TO ITEM 4 AND FOLLOW THE SCORE (SCORES 2, p. 24).

Exercise

1 Is the melody in the top part? If not, where is it?

2 What do you think the instruction *sost.* means in bars 10 and 12?

3 What significant 'landmark' occurs at bar 13?

Answers

1 The melody in the right hand is placed in an inner (i.e. lowest right-hand) part, corresponding to an alto voice in range. (This, incidentally, poses a particular difficulty for the pianist in that only the thumb and first two fingers can be employed for the melody.) The texture and spacing of the various parts result in a peculiarly subtle effect.

2 *Sost.* (*sostenuto*) is here used by Brahms instead of the more usual *ritenuto* (which means 'getting slower' – *ritardando* and *rallentando* mean the same) since the instruction is merely to hold back the tempo. You will notice that the injunction applies to only one chord at bar 12, and thus the word takes on a meaning more usually expressed by 'pause'. (*Fermata*, *sostenuto* and *tenuto* mean much the same in this context. Actually, in our recording, Radu Lupu observes the instruction at bar 10, but hardly at all in bar 12. Artistic licence!) Brahms was particularly addicted to these somewhat unusual shades of meaning for *sostenuto*, which is more normally used to indicate a style of playing (i.e. sustained).

3 Bar 13 marks a return to the opening melody and key, prepared for by the *sostenuto* and harmonic colouring of the previous bars.

Brahms was sufficiently patriotic to give this set of pieces a title in German. Our extract comes from the third of *Vier Klavierstücke* (Four Piano Pieces). Beethoven was among the first to depart from the customary Italian tempo markings, and the principle of using German directions was taken up by Wagner and others. Brahms and some of his nineteenth-century contemporaries felt less strongly about this, and on the whole preferred to write such markings in Italian. German nationalism, already apparent earlier in the nineteenth century, intensified after the 1870 Franco–Prussian War with the ensuing unification of Germany.

This brief reminder of the kind of score reading that you started in Unit 9 should, I hope, have posed few problems. If it did, however, go through the areas in which you had difficulty until your reading is reasonably fluent. Unit 9 also introduced you to the layout of three-stave textures, and Section 3 below offers a brief reminder of this, although you will probably find that the textures are far from easy.

Figure 2   Johannes Brahms (1833–97).

3   THREE-STAVE SCORE READING

3.1   DEBUSSY: *ONDINE*

Towards the end of the nineteenth century, composers occasionally used three staves for piano writing in an attempt to render the layout more practical and pleasing for both performer and reader. Some twentieth-century

piano music goes on to four, or even more, staves! In Scores 2 (p. 27) you will find bars 1–20 of Debussy's *Ondine*. Ondine was the seductive spirit of the deep who lured sailors to their deaths by her beautiful singing. The piece comes from Debussy's second book of Preludes, a set of twelve pieces published in 1913. Though brief, the extract will give you a flavour of Debussy's later style, with its irregular metres and fragmented melodies. You will also meet a few interpretative directions in French. The extract is recorded as Item 5 on the audio-cassette, and you will probably want to listen to it several times. Before you do, there are a number of features in the notation that I must mention.

You will notice that this music is written mostly on three staves. The purpose of this is to make the music more readable, but the layout does not in fact tell you which notes to play with which hand. To the performer the layout is, in this sense, less, rather than more, practical. However, we are reading, not playing. Look carefully in your score at the following points and use your highlighting pen for those that help you best.

1   The two-note chord[2] in bars 1 and 2 (middle stave) sounds *above* the previous **cluster** (a group of three or more notes on adjacent lines and spaces) although the latter is on a higher stave.

2   The middle stave in bars 3, 5 and elsewhere changes from bass to treble clef.

3   Note the fluctuating metre: $\frac{6}{8}$ to $\frac{9}{8}$ and *vice versa*.

4   Notice the notes in small type (known as grace notes) at bars 4, 6, 7 and elsewhere. These are played as quickly as possible before the notes they precede. You will meet them again in Unit 17.

5   Notice the *8...* sign at bars 8, 9 and later. Below this sign, the music sounds one octave higher than written. You will see this useful sign quite frequently in all types of music. Sometimes it is printed as *8va*, standing for 'ottava'.

6   Notice the italicized '3' at bars 4, 6 and 7, and '5' at bars 8 and 9. These are *triplets* and *quintuplets* respectively. (Note that *triplet* here does not mean three quavers or three crotchets.) In this extract the *3* indicates that a group of three semiquavers, rather than two, makes up one quaver. The *5* indicates that five demisemiquavers, rather than four, fit similarly into one quaver. (You might ask yourself about the *12, 10* and *9* groupings later in the extract.)

---

[2]   A two-note chord could alternatively be called an *interval,* as you know.

As you can see, there is quite a lot to take in here[3]. As a generality, when you follow the score your eye needs to dip down to take in the mainly very low notes on the bottom stave, which you could mark with your highlighting pen as convenient landmarks. The layout is basically: right hand for top stave, left hand for the middle stave, with very low notes on the added (bottom) stave. Now try following the score while you listen to the music.

  LISTEN TO ITEM 5 AND FOLLOW THE SCORE (SCORES 2, p.27).

Like Brahms, Debussy mixes his native language with Italian. (His Italian directions are *Scherzando* 'playfully' and *rubato*– literally 'robbed', though in practice the word signifies an expressive flexibility in the manner of play-

Figure 3 Claude Debussy (1862–1918).

ing.) Well done if you worked out that '*retenu … au Mouvement*' from bars 10–11 is the equivalent of the Italian '*rallentando … a tempo*'. The other directions are as follows.

scintillant	scintillating, twinkling (as of water)
doux	sweet(ly)
à l'aise	literally 'at ease', thus 'effortlessly'
léger	light(ly)
en dehors	literally 'on the outside', thus 'bring out' (the melody)

These are for reference only. You do not need to memorize them.

3.2   BACH: FANTASIA AND FUGUE IN G MINOR

The Debussy piece was none too easy, so now here are two less formidable examples of three-stave keyboard music. The first comes from an organ work of Bach, and consists of the first fourteen bars of the so-called Fantasia and Fugue in G minor (BWV542): there is no evidence that Bach intended the two pieces to be paired. The fugue was written first (between 1708 and 1717 during Bach's years in Weimar), whereas the preceding movement dates from his time at Cöthen, 1717–23. Although the extract in Scores 2 (p. 5) represents only just under one third of the Fantasia, it is characteristic of the movement as a whole in that flamboyant, rhetorical episodes (such as bars 1–8) alternate with imitative passages (such as bars 9–13). As our performance indulges in a certain amount of *tempo rubato* in the first eight bars (as is appropriate to a Fantasia), and the underlying bass line does not change until bar 8, you will not have the help of a regular pulse and prominent bass landmarks when you follow the score. This will give you some practice in following the intricacies of the score. As for the next six bars, I imagine that your eyes will be fixed mostly on the highest and lowest notes of the texture. Remember: you do not need to read *every* note in the score! (The dotted ties in bars 9–11 are editorial.)

   LISTEN TO ITEM 6 AND FOLLOW THE SCORE (SCORES 2. p. 5).

---

[3]   In fact, this extract is quite difficult, so if you get lost, go on to Section 3.2 and come back to the Debussy piece towards the end of the week.

3.3 FROM BACH TO LISZT

The next extract (also for organ) comes from Liszt's *Präludium und Fuge über den Namen BACH* (*Prelude and Fugue on the name of BACH*). Originally written in 1855, the work was revised by Liszt in 1870 and this is the version usually heard today. (He also provided a fine piano arrangement of the piece.) I have supplied the music and score of the opening 41 bars, which should be sufficient to indicate the radical nature of Liszt's harmonic language and motivic treatment of material.[4]

Before you see and hear the music, though, I should explain that, as indicated in the chart on p. 77 of Units 1–3, German musical notation uses the letter B for B♭, and H for B♮. You can see, therefore, that the name BACH transforms itself into a rather striking chromatic motive:

B   A   C   H

Bach himself had noticed that his name could be spelt musically, and turned this to account in several of his later works. A number of composers subsequently made use of the BACH motive as a kind of peg on which to write a piece of music. This is what Liszt does in his Prelude and Fugue, which is not a portrait of his distinguished musical ancestor, but a substantial piece based on the BACH four-note motive. The work thus represents yet another aspect of variation technique, which you came across in Part 1 of Unit 10. Incidentally, the organist on our recording draws a 16-foot manual stop up to bar 29, and thus a rather grand sound results: the notes on the page are duplicated at the lower octave.[5]

The extract is supplied in Scores 2 in two forms: unannotated (p. 38) and annotated (p. 40). In the first instance you should look at the unannotated version. It is recorded as Item 7.

---

[4] This will be discussed further in the second half of the course, when you start to study Romantic music in more detail.

[5] An 8-foot stop indicates that notes played on this rank of pipes are at sounding pitch. By mathematical analogy, playing on a 16-foot pipe will result in notes sounding an octave lower (rather like a double-bass part). 4-foot and 2-foot pipes sound one and two octaves higher respectively.

 LISTEN TO ITEM 7 WHILE FOLLOWING THE SCORE (SCORES 2, p. 38).

If you got lost, there are several points you can highlight in the score: the return of BACH in dotted minims at bar 13 (top stave); the pedal entry at bar 16, and again at 24. Now try following the score again, two or three times.

Exercise

Now take your score, and mark in all the appearances you can find of the BACH motive. (You will notice that in the pedal part of bars 1–4 the motive could be more properly called an *ostinato*. Refer back to Unit 10, Section 2, if you need to, for the definition of this term.) Then – and this is much more difficult – see how many transposed versions of the motive you can find. This is where your knowledge of intervals will be useful, since on each occasion the motive must be delineated by the intervals

semitone down, minor third up, semitone down

These intervals will always be the same whether or not the motive begins on the note B♭. (Remember that four notes in succession result in *three* intervals.) Watch out for the double sharps in bar 9!

Answer

The answer is given in the annotated version in Scores 2 (p. 40). The straight lines and arrows indicate the BACH motif in its original form; the wiggly lines and arrows indicate the various transposed forms.

 CHECK YOUR ANSWER WITH SCORES 2, p. 40.

I hope you managed to discover many of the BACH motives in the original form; if you traced only half of the transposed versions, this represents a considerable achievement.

Exercise

As light relief after all this hard work, you might care to think of a word meaning 'flesh of ox, bull or cow', and another word meaning 'a common green vegetable'. On one occasion, both words acted as *stimuli* to the imagination of the Irish composer John Field (1782–1837), while improvising at a party. All the letters of both words are contained in the seven notes of the scale, in the (British) notational system. However, do not spend more than five minutes on this!

Answer

 Beef and cabbage! Field used these notes for his improvisation. Try this yourself and see whether your recipe is tasty!

3.4   A PRELIMINARY CHECKLIST

One rather basic point might well be worrying you at this stage. Indeed, you may perhaps have been concerned about it right from the beginning of the course. It is this: should you be able to hear the music on the page in your head before you hear it played?

A simple folk song or the top line of a hymn tune – yes, if possible. For anything more complicated: probably not – even some experienced musicians cannot. But you should be aware of generalities: texture, dynamics, tempo and **tessitura**. (Tessitura is a useful word, referring to the general 'lie' of a vocal, or sometimes instrumental, part: high, medium or low in its general range, for example. In Italian the word actually means 'texture', something rather different, of course.) So when you hear the music and follow the score, you then marry these elements to the notational (and other) symbols on the page. If this is happening to some extent, then at this stage you are doing well. Actually, it can be quite fun to try to imagine the sounds first, and then compare this with a recorded performance. If you can get a general sense of the feel of the music through score reading, you can look into the details of individual notes or chords afterwards with a better understanding.

You should now break off from the unit text in order to work through Video Section 1. The music examples that occur in the video are reproduced here for your convenience, along with their associated notes.

4   THE ALTO CLEF

 VIDEO NOTES
UNIT 14, VIDEO SECTION 1

Introduction

The object of this video section is to familiarize you with the alto clef and to give you some practice in writing in it. The music examples that occur in the video section are reproduced in the Summary below.

NOW WATCH THE VIDEO SECTION. YOU WILL NEED MANUSCRIPT PAPER.

During the video section

The first time you are asked to stop the tape, write a descending scale of C major in semibreves, using the alto clef, starting on middle C and covering one octave. The answer is printed as Video Example 3 in the Summary below.

The second time you are asked to stop the tape, write an ascending scale of C major in semibreves, using the alto clef, starting on middle C and covering a range of an octave and a fifth. (That is, write the scale from middle C to the C an octave above, and then continued to the G above that.) The answer is printed as Video Example 4 in the Summary below.

Summary

Unlike the treble clef, which exists basically in one shape, there are various forms of alto clef which you may come across. Three are shown below. The one on the left is probably the easiest to write, and the one in the middle is used in print. The one on the right is not shown in the video section, but is sometimes used in hand-written music.

Video Example 1   Some C clefs

The clef is 'anchored' around middle C, which is fixed to the middle line of the stave:

Video Example 2

middle C

Here is a descending scale of C major, written in the alto clef and starting from middle C:

Video Example 3   Descending scale of C major

And similarly, an ascending scale from middle C, going on to the G an octave and a fifth above middle C:

Video Example 4   Ascending scale of C, continued a fifth higher

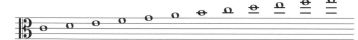

As an exercise in reading the alto clef, you might like to follow the viola part in your score of Beethoven's Fifth Symphony whilst listening to the music. (See 'After the video section' below.)

Here is the British national anthem complete, first written out in the familiar treble clef:

Video Example 5   The British national anthem

If you were to write this tune an octave lower, in the register where a man would sing it, using either the treble or bass clefs, you would need several leger lines. As you can see below, use of the alto clef requires no leger lines at this octave.

Video Example 6   The British national anthem (alto clef)

After the video section

You may wish to play this Video Example 5 on your keyboard. (If you are feeling really confident, try it an octave lower, using the alto clef – i.e. Video Example 6.)

You may also wish to listen to part of the first movement of Beethoven's Fifth Symphony (Audio-cassette 16, Side 2) while following the viola line in your score.

 PLAY OR FOLLOW THE ITEMS MENTIONED ABOVE IF YOU WISH.

5 STRING WRITING ON UP TO THREE STAVES

5.1 MOZART'S DUOS

You met three-stave writing in Unit 9: two violins and cello, the *concertino* group in the Baroque concerto grosso. There, the clefs employed are generally two treble and one bass, although if you have scrutinized your score of the Corelli Concerto Grosso, Op. 6 No. 4 (Scores 1), you will have noticed another clef in the cello part from time to time, one that we shall be dealing with in the second video section for this unit. But I am going to start with two extracts from pieces written for two stringed instruments only: the violin and the viola, so that you can gain some additional practice in coping with the alto clef.

Between July and October 1783, Mozart came to the rescue of Haydn's brother Michael, also a composer, who had been commissioned to write some duets for violin and viola, but was taken ill while working on them. Mozart composed two works to make up Michael Haydn's set of six, and these two are generally recognized as being the finest works ever written for this slender medium. Listen to the opening of the *Rondeau* of the first Duo in G major, K423[6], Item 8 on your audio-cassette, following the music in Example 3.

 LISTEN TO ITEM 8 WHILE FOLLOWING EXAMPLE 3.

You can see that the viola takes up the main theme of the movement at bar 9, repeating an octave lower what the violin plays at the beginning.

Next, to give you some practice in the reading of short note values, Example 4 is the opening slow introduction to the second Duo, in B♭, K424. As in the work in G major, you can see and hear that the two instruments are of equal importance in terms of melody and figurations. This is Item 9 on your audio-cassette.

Example 3   Mozart: Duo in G major, K423, Rondeau, bars 1–18

---

[6]   The Köchel numbers of Mozart's works (e.g. K423) refer to the catalogue of Mozart's compositions *Chronologisch-thematisches Verzeichnis sämtlicher Tonwerke Wolfgang Amade Mozarts* (1862), compiled by Ludwig Köchel (1800–77). Important revisions to Köchel's chronology have been included in subsequent editions: second, 1905; third, 1937 and sixth, 1964.

LISTEN TO ITEM 9 WHILE FOLLOWING EXAMPLE 4.

Example 4   Mozart: Duo in B♭ major, K424, Introduction, bars 1–10

5.2   HANDEL: OP. 6 NO. 12

Now for some orchestral music on three staves: a complete movement from Handel's Concerto Grosso in B minor, the last of a set of twelve concertos, Op. 6, published in 1740. This is printed in Scores 2 (p. 28). As you can see, each 'line' of music consists of three staves, bracketed together on the left. A group of staves, such as these, which together comprise a single line of music, is called a **system**.

You will notice that the piece is cast in the form of a binary slow movement, each half repeated, with a written-out variation on each repeated half. (The *concertino*, by the way, plays with the *ripieno* in this movement, a not uncommon feature in Handel's string concertos.) Listen to the movement several times in order to become familiar with the style. Part of that style in our recording encompasses such matters as the occasional melodic decoration at cadences and additional notes in the melody when it is repeated. Listen for the continuo too.

Looking through a movement should be your first priority with any new piece you score-read. Then you partly look, partly listen, for confirmation of the notes you expect to hear. Increasingly, your expectations will come from a familiarity with the style: late Baroque, early Beethoven, Vivaldi, or whatever. This works for me, and you should find it helpful. Apart from these considerations, it is all excellent ear-training. So in the Handel extract, follow the top part the first time, then each of the other two parts for your subsequent playings. This is Item 10 on the audio-cassette. (Note that the final repeat mark in the score is probably a printer's error and is not observed in our recording.)

 LISTEN TO ITEM 10 WHILE FOLLOWING THE SCORE (SCORES 2, p. 28).

The distribution of the strings is rather unusual in this movement. Handel divides the violins into three rather than two, and instructs the first and second violins to play in unison, and the third violins to play similarly with the violas. Perhaps Handel wanted a particularly strong top line, since the melody is undoubtedly one of his finest; certainly he made a conscious choice about the kind of balance he wanted. As a result of this scoring, the violas never play in the bottom fifth of their compass. You

Figure 4   George Frideric Handel (1685– 1759), by Thomas Hudson, 1756.

may perhaps have wondered about the key of this movement. The work from which it is taken is in the key of B minor. The fact that this movement is in E major indicates that it must be a *middle* movement, since the first and (usually) last movements will be in the key of the work as a whole.

I hope that you are by now managing to take in the alto clef more easily; as I remarked on the video section, try to follow the general line of the part rather than attempt to hear it as such in your head.

5.3   MOZART: DIVERTIMENTO IN E FLAT (1)

One type of chamber ensemble occasionally found *c*.1750, and more frequently towards the end of the eighteenth century, was the string trio. Its most usual combination was one each of violin, viola and cello. (In the Baroque, the popular equivalent was the trio sonata, with two violins and cello.) Yet again, Mozart provided one of the most magnificent examples in his Divertimento in E♭, K563. His choice of title reflects the fact that the

work is not cast in the usual three or four movements, as would normally be the case with a string trio, but in six large-scale movements. The divertimento – or serenade, cassation or notturno, which in the late-eighteenth century were all more-or-less interchangeable titles – was usually distinguished from symphonies, sonatas and related genres by its proliferation of movements. These betray the origins of the divertimento as 'background' or 'entertainment' music. The two pieces in Scores 2, pp. 44 and 46, are short extracts from this work. First, we shall look at the extract from the fourth movement, beginning on p. 46 of Scores 2. This is recorded as Item 11. The recording begins on the last quaver of bar 176, just before the word *Maggiore*.

  LISTEN TO ITEM 11 SEVERAL TIMES WHILE FOLLOWING THE SCORE (SCORES 2, p. 46).

You may have wondered about two points here. First, the key is obviously B♭, not E♭. So, as in the Handel extract, this movement is not in the home key – a clear indication that this is one of the work's *inner* movements. Second, the word *Maggiore* means *major*. Composers frequently write this after a clearly defined section in a minor key (often one variation of a set, as is the case here). It is not really necessary, as it is always obvious when minor becomes major.

Exercise

 I am sure that you now know what important landmarks to look for, but in order to put your thoughts into words, write two or three sentences describing the various types of rhythms in that extract.

Answer

Up to bar 199 the viola, playing mostly in minims and crotchets, acts as an anchor for the two accompanying instruments: it plays a sort of *cantus firmus*. Around it the violin and cello play in shorter note values. At bar 200, the viola takes up the violin's rapid figurations, and the cello does likewise at 204. During the last six bars the busyness gradually subsides in order to lead naturally to the tranquil ending.

I hope that you managed to formulate something on those lines, but even if you did not, as long as you are managing to follow these scores successfully, then you are achieving the aims of this unit. In addition to the suggestions I have made already, it is always a good idea to look through the score first, trying to determine what and where the landmarks are in advance, so that you have a score reading plan in your mind before you begin to listen. And try, if you can, to look a few beats ahead of the music when you are listening. It makes you feel good! It is also very practical: you don't have time to react once you have heard the sound!

If you feel reasonably happy about all this then you are evidently scanning the more important aspects of the texture. You know when to move your eyes from one instrumental line to another as different instruments become prominent; and you are not, I trust, attempting in the Mozart Divertimento to follow every note in the cello part – and certainly not, I hope, every note in the violin line! Perhaps you are aware too of such matters as the harmonic rhythm, dynamics, and so on. Keep an eye open for such technicalities as **double stopping**, where a bow is drawn simultaneously across either two adjacent stopped strings or across an open and an adjacent stopped string. You look for this in string writing by identifying two notes played simultaneously; if the notes have separate stems and beams (as in the violin part at bar 203) then the part-writing is likely to be contrapuntal.

Even in this relatively simple piece, the landmarks to look out for change constantly, and it is impossible to give you detailed hints appropriate to every score. If you become lost, go back to the beginning. In any event, persevere, and keep practising until your reading is reasonably fluent. Remember that the first requirement is to keep pace with the pulse: a useful preliminary exercise is to tap in time with the music before you look at the score. Then, next time, try moving your finger across the score at that speed.

5.4 MOZART: DIVERTIMENTO IN E FLAT (2)

The next extract is longer, since it comprises the exposition section of the first movement of the Mozart Divertimento. You will need to play this several times if only, as I suggested in Section 5.2, to gain some familiarity with the style. Try it three times, following each individual instrumental part in the score (Scores 2, p. 44); then a fourth time, moving your eyes from one line to another as the interesting areas of the music continually interchange. Look especially at bars 9–11 and 27–34 where you may experience some perceptual difficulties when the parts cross. In bars 9–11, the viola plays above the violin; in bars 27–34, the cello is the middle part, playing above

the viola. Actually, in bars 27–34 the cello part uses the tenor clef, which I shall consider in the second video section, so for these bars, to avoid confusion, keep your eyes on the violin part.

This extract is recorded as Item 12.

NOW LISTEN TO ITEM 12 WHILE FOLLOWING THE SCORE (SCORES 2, p. 44).

Item 12 illustrates well the nature of part-crossing, a frequent problem in score reading, especially in chamber music. These *perceptual* difficulties are mostly *reading* difficulties: when the violin sounds *beneath* the viola, or the viola *beneath* the cello, it can be confusing. You may find that you take this in your stride, but it is quite common even for good readers to feel disconcerted if the cello, which we instinctively associate with the bass part, perhaps sounds higher than the violin. The highest sounding notes in the composite web of sound appear visually at the very bottom of the score.

Now try following this extract again, moving your eyes from one instrument in the score to another, as the need arises, and taking in as many of the features I have mentioned as you can.

NOW LISTEN AGAIN TO ITEM 12 WHILE FOLLOWING THE SCORE (SCORES 2, p. 44).

Exercise

I have already mentioned two examples of part-crossing. Look at bars 53–73 of the score, and list all the places where one part crosses another for most of one bar or more.

Answer

1 Bars 55–7: viola mostly above violin.

2 Bars 58–61: cello mostly above viola (and in 60–1 above violin too).

3 Bars 66–7: cello above viola.

Use your highlighting pen to mark these in your score – listen again if you wish. You may find part-crossing referred to as 'overlapping', but this can have a different, though related, meaning in strict part-writing. If there is anything that confuses you in this section, go through it again, repeating the first video section if necessary.

6 FOUR-PART STRING TEXTURES

6.1 PREAMBLE

I trust that you are feeling somewhat more confident about your ability to read fairly complex three-stave textures than at the start of the week. I hope that the various landmarks – ever different in each piece of music you come across – are becoming self-evident. I assume that you are training yourself to glance up and down (what I have called 'scanning') whilst reading from left to right in the normal way. With the more difficult scores you have met in this unit, if you needed to read through them three or four times before feeling confident about following them, that is fine; I have suggested you should do this anyway. Constant and regular practice is the surest way to success.

The remainder of Unit 14 ought to pose few problems, since we shall be concerned simply with one more C clef and the addition of further staves to the score: four staves in Section 6, and five in Sections 8 and 9. Although the C clefs are new to you, they should not create difficulties in your score reading. Try not to think of them as 'special' when following a score. Simply take in the contours of the notes on the C-clef staves, if these are the parts you are following. You are usually not concerned with the names of the notes, so it does not matter if you cannot name them instantly.

6.2 JOSEPH HAYDN (1732–1809)

For four-part string textures, one inevitably thinks of the string quartet, one of the most frequent chamber genres, written for 2 violins, viola and cello. Its score may therefore *look* the same as that of a string section of an orchestra. In fact the string quartet may be regarded as the chamber analogy of the symphony, and the Classical equivalent of the Baroque trio sonata, which, as you know, has four players. The origins of the string quartet can be traced in various ways, but in Austria the entertainment music of serenade and divertimento (see Section 5.3) were important precursors of the string quartet. (The scoring of Mozart's Divertimento for string *trio* may well seem slightly confusing in this context, unfortunately!) Early quartets frequently included two minuet movements, reflecting the importance of dance elements in popular entertainment music.

Haydn is frequently called 'the father of the symphony'; this is inaccurate, since there were numerous symphonic composers before Haydn. It might be more appropriate to describe him as the 'father of the string quartet'; there were some isolated examples of earlier quartets than his, but Haydn's are still the earliest to be played regularly. If 'the most striking innovation of Haydn's string quartet writing [is] its air of conversation'[7] – which is another way of saying that all four instruments contribute equally to the musical discourse – then that in itself indicates that any coherent score reading presupposes an ability to follow the thematic points of interest in the score as they move from one instrument to another. Our scores, then, are beginning to get more complicated, as we shall soon see with succeeding examples from quartets by Haydn and Beethoven.

Figure 5   Joseph Haydn (1732–1809) by Thomas Hardy, 1791.

[7] Charles Rosen, *The Classical Style*, London, 1971, p. 141.

6.3   HAYDN: OP. 1 NO. 1

First, a complete movement from Haydn's very first quartet, 'La Chasse' (The Hunt), No. 1 of a set of six published as Op. 1 in the late 1750s, when Haydn was in his mid-twenties. Scores 2, p. 35, gives the second movement of the work, a minuet and trio – very useful since, if you do get lost, each half of both minuet and trio will be repeated. (You looked at the structure of the Minuet/Scherzo and Trio in Unit 10, Section 5.) When the minuet returns after the trio, it is, in our recording, played straight through without repeats. This return will also be useful as a point of reference if need be! It is recorded as Item 13.

In the score, the first two staves are for first and second violins, the third stave is for the viola, and the bottom stave is for the cello. This is the standard layout of a string-quartet score; you may like to write the instrumentation into the score.

 LISTEN NOW TO ITEM 13 WHILE FOLLOWING THE SCORE (SCORES 2, p. 35).

Perhaps by this stage you have the confidence to pick out some different harmonic textures, noticing them by both eye and ear, and relating the two. For example: in bars 1–10, the parallel sixths or thirds between the violins; in the same bars, the octaves between viola and cello; in bars 18–22, the unisons between the two upper parts and the octaves between the two lower parts; and in much of the trio, the broken chord figurations[8] in the two upper parts.[9] Perhaps you also feel that Rosen's earlier comment applied most of all to the trio, where the two upper and two lower parts converse with one another in a delightful manner. In the minuet proper, the interest lies mostly in the top part, and this is typical of the genre at this early stage in its evolution. (You will be studying the other minuet from this quartet in Unit 16.)

[8]   See Unit 9, Section 2.3.

[9]   Note that the octaves and unisons in this context are not 'wrong', since the texture is a 3-part one.

6.4   HAYDN: OP. 76 NO. 4

Next, an extract from the last movement of a much later Haydn quartet, the fourth of a set of six works published as Op. 76 in 1797, when Haydn was at the height of his powers. The score is in Scores 2, p. 36. The quartet is nicknamed 'The Sunrise', owing to a 'rising' theme and the leisurely and expansive treatment of the material at the very opening of the whole work. I have chosen the finale to give you some practice in reading a fast piece of music. In fact, the tempo changes twice from the initial *Allegro, ma non troppo* (Lively but not too much so), although our extract begins at the first increase in speed: *Più* (More) *allegro*; the next is at bar 129: *Più presto*. This is Item 14 on the audio-cassette.

Follow the extract several times. You will probably be able to concentrate exclusively on the first violin part (except between bars 114–118) but try following a different part on each playing. If you get lost, useful landmarks are the *Più presto* at bar 129, the viola and cello entry at bar 143, the climactic chord of E♭ at bar 156, and the semibreve Cs at bar 167. Mark these points in your score now.

 LISTEN TO ITEM 14 WHILE FOLLOWING THE SCORE (SCORES 2, p. 36).

You might well have detected a different kind of sound in this quartet, compared with that of Op. 1 No. 1, even allowing that Haydn's musical language is some 40 years older. There is still 'an air of conversation', but the conversation now appears to be taking place in a large (concert) room rather than a small chamber. The 'public' nature of Haydn's later quartets makes them very different in scope and mood from his earlier ones, and is symptomatic of the development of the genre over the previous 40 years. This quartet demonstrates that by now Haydn was also an assured and experienced symphonist. If you are at all familiar with Mozart's Italian operas, such as *The Marriage of Figaro* and *Don Giovanni,* you may perhaps have been reminded of the *buffo* (comic) finales of those works. *Buffo* in this context refers to the combination of a lively, often comic, ensemble in which an *accelerando* lends great excitement to the complex textures and also indicates to the audience that the close of the act is in sight. Haydn greatly admired Mozart's operas, especially *The Marriage of Figaro*: indeed Mozart's success in opera deterred Haydn from attempting to compete in this genre after Mozart's death in 1791.

6.5 BEETHOVEN: OP. 131

Finally, to one of the late string quartets of Beethoven, that in C♯ minor, Op. 131. This was written in 1826 and Beethoven regarded it as his finest quartet. There are two extracts in Scores 2, on pp. 21 and 22. We shall look first at the extract beginning on p. 22. It consists of bars 235–326 from the very witty and Haydnesque Presto movement. This will require on your part accurate scanning and an ability to read at speed. The composer's precise dynamic markings will be of some help, in addition to such landmarks as the viola and cello tune beginning at bar 259, and the high soaring first violin line at bars 287–306. Notice also the changing of the melody from high to low instruments: high from 235–50; low from 259–75. Beethoven's comment *Ritmo di quattro battute* indicates that in these sections the phrases are in four-bar groups, a proceeding dictated by the very fast tempo. Or, if you like, a group of four bars can be regarded as one 'big' bar, and there are four 'big' beats to this bar. *Piacevole* at the start of the extract means 'pleasingly'. Highlight all these points before you listen.

LISTEN TO ITEM 15 WHILE FOLLOWING THE SCORE (SCORES 2, p. 22).

The next extract (Scores 2, p. 21) is bars 231–53 from the preceding movement, a sublime set of variations. Note particularly the rich texture of bars 243–9, where the second violin and viola play the theme in octaves, enriched further by the viola's double stopping. At the same time, the first violin and cello add fragmented filigree passage-work around this tune. You will notice in bars 235–6 of the cello part that we meet our tenor clef again (the subject of the next video section). The notes at this point are middle C and the B one semitone below.

The extract is recorded as Item 16.

LISTEN TO ITEM 16 WHILE FOLLOWING THE SCORE (SCORES 2, p. 21).

Make sure that you are thoroughly familiar with this extract before you continue. If you are, you should now turn to the second video section for this

unit, where I shall talk briefly about this second C clef, as well as introduce you to string music on five staves. The music examples in Section 7 occur on the video and are included here for your convenience, along with some brief notes.

7 THE TENOR CLEF

 VIDEO NOTES
UNIT 14, VIDEO SECTION 2

Introduction

The object of this section of video is to familiarize you with the tenor clef, and to give you some practice in writing in it. The music examples that occur in the video section are reproduced in the Summary below.

NOW WATCH THE VIDEO SECTION. YOU WILL NEED MANUSCRIPT PAPER.

During the video section

The first time you are asked to stop the tape, write an ascending scale of C major in semibreves, using the tenor clef, starting on middle C and covering one octave. The answer is printed as Video Example 11 in the Summary below.

The second time you are asked to stop the tape, write the British national anthem in the tenor clef, starting on the G below middle C. You are shown the first two bars in the video section. Video Example 15 in the Summary below gives the tune an octave higher, in the treble clef, for reference. Video Example 16 shows the required tenor-clef version.

Summary

As with the alto clef, there are various versions of the tenor clef. Three are shown below. The one on the left is probably the easiest to write, and the one in the middle is used in print. The one on the right is not shown in the video section, but is sometimes used in hand-written music.

Video Example 7   Some tenor clefs

The tenor clef is 'anchored' around middle C which here is fixed to the fourth stave line from the bottom:

Video Example 8

middle C

This clef is sometimes referred to as C4, because the fourth line up is C. Thus the notes below are middle C (twice), and the B a semitone below (twice):

Video Example 9

middle C   B

Here is a descending scale of C major, starting on middle C:

Video Example 10   Descending scale of C

And similarly an ascending scale, starting from the same note:

Video Example 11   Ascending scale of C

The pitch range frequently found with this clef is from the C an octave below middle C to that an octave above:

Video Example 12   Usual range for tenor clef

Here is an extract from the second movement of Tchaikovsky's *Serenade for Strings*.

Video Example 13   Tchaikovsky, Serenade for Strings, *second movement, extract*

If the tenor-clef melody in bars 182–9 of Video Example 13 is re-written in a mixture of treble and bass clefs, it looks much more angular:

Video Example 14   Tchaikovsky, Serenade for Strings, *tenor-clef melody re-written in treble and bass clefs*

Here is the British national anthem written in conventional treble-clef notation:

Video Example 15   The British national anthem

The first note of the British national anthem in the tenor clef is:

Here is the complete tune in the tenor clef:

Video Example 16   British national anthem in the tenor clef

The sharp key signatures in the tenor clef show a different pattern from those in the alto clef (and indeed from those in the treble and bass clefs). However, the flats are grouped in the normal way:

Video Example 17   Various key signatures in alto and tenor clefs

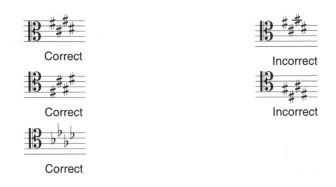

Correct

Incorrect

Correct

Incorrect

Correct

8   FIVE-PART STRING TEXTURES

8.1   PREAMBLE

The remainder of this unit should, I hope, be fairly straightforward. Any problems that may arise because of the inclusion of a fifth stave should iron themselves out with regular practice and the gradual accumulation of other musical skills. Keep practising the score-reading work: it all repays repetition.

8.2   THE STRING QUINTET

Five-part string textures lead logically to the string quintet and string orchestra. As you would expect, the string quintet adds one further instrument to the string quartet. This can be either a second viola or a second cello. (Exceptionally, Dvorak's Quintet, Op. 77, adds a double bass to the normal string quartet.) The first great string quintets were written by Mozart who, as a viola player himself, favoured the scoring of two violins, two violas and one cello. Of the six authentic quintets, four are acknowledged masterpieces.

The additional instrument offered Mozart, and all subsequent quintet composers, far greater scope for textural variety than was possible in the string quartet. The nineteenth century was not a propitious era for chamber music, since composers tended to concern themselves with new forms, new types of orchestral colouring, increasing instrumental virtuosity, and so on. Such developments were not conducive to the writing of chamber music. Relatively few great composers were attracted to the medium, although the quality of such works as were written was high. Mendelssohn and Brahms each produced two string quintets, laid out on the principles of Mozart's scoring.

8.3   THE SCHUBERT QUINTET

A smaller number of composers favoured the combination of two violins, one viola and two cellos. One of the first to write for this arrangement was Luigi Boccherini (1743–1805), a contemporary of Haydn, and himself a virtuoso cellist. However, the great masterpiece in this form is undoubtedly the work in C by Schubert, written in the autumn of 1828, just a few weeks before the composer's death. Our next two examples are taken from this quintet. First, bars 1–15 of the slow movement, whose outer sections represent some of the serenest music that Schubert ever wrote. The extract is recorded as Item 17 and, printed on p. 56 of Scores 2. Listen to it first without the score so as to familiarize yourself with the style.

 LISTEN TO ITEM 17.

Now look at your score, and make sure you know precisely where the four ♩. beats in these long $\frac{12}{8}$ bars occur. In bar 1 (whose rhythmic patterns are the same for the next five bars) the beats work out as shown below (the dashed lines show the subdivision of the bar into four ♩. beats).

You could put the beats into your score if you wish. (You might also like to write in the instrumentation. The first two staves are for first and second violins respectively; the middle stave is the viola, and the bottom two staves are for first and second cellos.)

Now listen to the extract a second time, following the first violin part in the score. (The recording ends at the point marked with an arrow in the score.)

 LISTEN TO ITEM 17 AGAIN WHILE FOLLOWING THE SCORE (SCORES 2, p. 56).

That, I hope, was not too difficult. But I am certain that before too long you noticed that the 'core' of the music is actually in the middle of the texture: in the second violin, assisted by the viola. The other instruments act in an accompanying role. Now listen to the extract again, this time following the second violin and viola parts, but trying to take in the first violin interjections as well. Then, in a final run, try to be aware of the *pizzicato* role of the second cello.

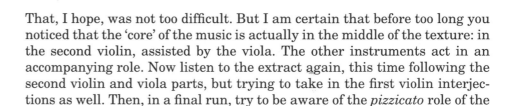 LISTEN TO ITEM 17 AGAIN WHILE FOLLOWING THE SCORE (SCORES 2, p. 56).

Next, we shall look at and listen to the opening of the first movement, which begins on page 54 of Scores 2. This will give you some practice in coping with both alto and tenor clefs. This extract is more complex, and again raises the problem of deciding where to look in the score. Generally speaking, it is best to look for the tune or perhaps some prominent accompanimental figure immediately preceding a tune. As always, this will become more obvious to you the more score reading you practise. This is what I should look out for in this example:

First violin, bars 1–10.

First cello, bars 11–19.

First violin, bars 20–35.

Both cellos, bars 35–49.

Viola and first cello, bars 49–56.

Both cellos, bars 58–79.

Both violins thereafter.

It might be a good idea to take your highlighting pen and mark these bar references in your score now. Or use a pencil to put boxes around the bars quoted above. The extract is quite complicated; you will need to try it several times. This is Item 18 on the audio-cassette.

LISTEN TO ITEM 18 WHILE FOLLOWING THE SCORE (SCORES 2, p. 54).

You may well have found that extract rather difficult. At bar 11 the first cello sounds above all the other instruments; in bars 60–79 the two cellos start to play above the viola, which is providing a *pizzicato* bass part. Such textural complexities and awkward crossing of parts make this extract perhaps the most difficult this week. Even if you found it hard going, you are doing very well. I have deliberately placed it at this point in the unit, so you should, with luck, be able to coast towards the end without too many problems.

8.4 · THE MENDELSSOHN QUINTETS

The increasing size of orchestras in the nineteenth century was paralleled by the increasingly orchestral nature of much of the chamber music written. This is not a criticism, by the way, but merely an observation of the attitude taken by many Romantic composers towards the writing of chamber music. The next two extracts, from the two quintets of Mendelssohn (1809–47), illustrate this trend clearly. First, the second theme in the finale of Mendelssohn's First Quintet in A, Op.18, of 1826, beginning on p. 42 of Scores 2. You will see that there are two staves using the alto clef; these are for the first and second violas. You may like to write the instrumentation into the score. Often miniature scores give the instrumentation at the beginning of a movement only.

We pick the music up just before the second theme, at bar 34 (indicated in the score by an arrow), with the second subject coming up at bar 50. The recording ends at the second arrow (bar 94). This is Item 19 on the audio-cassette.

LISTEN TO ITEM 19 WHILE FOLLOWING THE SCORE (SCORES 2, p. 42).

I hope you found that less difficult than the Schubert. To me, the textures are easier to follow, not least because most of the interest is in the top part. The frequent use of *tremolando*[10] in the four lower parts (for example, bars 42–9) is typical of the orchestral nature of much Romantic chamber music. This important stylistic feature is one of many that make nineteenth-century chamber music so different from that of the previous century.

And to follow, another very similar example: the last page of the slow movement of Mendelssohn's Second Quintet in B♭, Op. 87, of 1845 (Scores 2, p. 43). This movement is in D minor – related to the principal key of B♭ – and is in sonata form (you may wish to refer back to Unit 10, Section 7, to remind yourself of the sonata principle). The extract begins with the recapitulation of the second subject in the tonic major at bar 70. On the page this looks very orchestral for chamber music, but nevertheless it works extremely well in performance, and as a climactic peroration has few parallels in nineteenth-century music. Here, the *tremolando* (bars 78–88) is unmeasured, that is, the notes are to be played as fast as possible, whereas in the previous extract the tremolando was measured – that is, 'spelt out' in undulating semiquavers. You will notice that for the first seven bars the cello has the highest part in the texture. And *attacca* (attack) under the last bar indicates that the finale follows without a break. This extract is recorded as Item 20.

LISTEN TO ITEM 20 WHILE FOLLOWING THE SCORE (SCORES 2, p. 43).

You may have noticed that a fifth instrument does not necessarily make a great difference in the complexity of a quintet, compared with a quartet. Quite often only four instruments are in fact playing at any one time, and indeed the best quintet writing aims at 'letting air' into the music whenever possible. On the other hand, the three lowest instruments of a quintet – whatever their combination – can provide rich textures of a kind impossible in a quartet.

---

[10] On stringed instruments, a **tremolando** (also **tremolo**) refers to very rapid repetitions of the same notes(s) produced by quickly alternating bow directions. An **unmeasured tremolo**, indicated by three or more beams across the stem of the note(s), is one where the notes don't have precisely defined durations. In Item 19 the tremolo is of a kind where there are repetitions of pairs of notes; this is known as a **slurred tremolo**. It is also a measured **tremolo** (that is, the notes are played as precise semiquavers). Similarly, there can also be a measured tremolo (on one note) and an unmeasured slurred tremolo (on a pair of notes). The slurred tremolo is also found in piano music.

in a string quartet, should the composer wish to exploit the deep, dark areas of the pitch range lying beneath the violins' low G string.

Figure 6   Felix Mendelssohn (1809–47). Engraving by J. W. Cook.

8.5   TCHAIKOVSKY: *SERENADE FOR STRINGS*

Now we come to a work at which we have not looked very closely so far, Tchaikovsky's *Serenade for Strings*, Op. 48. Items 21–3 are taken from three of its movements, and are in approximate order of score-reading difficulty. You should have your own copy of the score of this work. (You may need to look back to the start of the work to remind yourself that the staves represent, reading downwards, first violins, second violins, violas, cellos and double basses.)

First, bars 1–38 of the *Elégie* (third movement); this by now should pose no problems. The melodic interest is in the first violin part up to bar 30, after which it is transferred to violas and cellos playing in unison. The last five bars of this extract are a good illustration of a unison melody in the two C clefs: to the eye, the lines appear to be a third apart, which as you now know, is far from being the case! This is recorded as Item 21 on the audio-cassette.

  LISTEN NOW TO ITEM 21 AND FOLLOW IT IN YOUR SCORE (THIRD MOVEMENT, BARS 1–38).

Next, bars 1–73 of the second movement, a waltz. This is only slightly harder than the previous extract. At the point where the tune is taken up by the cellos and second violins in octaves (in bars 53–73) you will have some good practice in reading the tenor clef. (You might try playing this tune on your keyboard, reading from the tenor clef at bar 57.) This extract is recorded as Item 22.

 LISTEN NOW TO ITEM 22 WHILE FOLLOWING THE SCORE (SECOND MOVEMENT, BARS 1–73).

PLAY THE TUNE IF YOU WISH.

Finally, bars 1–83 of the finale (fourth movement), a rondo preceded by a slow introduction. The latter should by now be child's play, though the 'Allegro con spirito' needs a quick brain. In fact, the greatest difficulty in this movement is not the textures, simply the fast tempo. You may therefore find it helpful at a preliminary hearing to follow the first beats of each bar with your finger, since the speed, though rapid, is at least constant. If anything, try to look ahead of the music. In really fast movements, this is almost essential. In bar 43 the instruction *alzate sordini* means 'remove the mutes'.[11] As this is the last exercise in the week, I will leave you to find the appropriate highlights for yourself. This is recorded as Item 23 on the audio-cassette.

  LISTEN TO ITEM 23 AND FOLLOW YOUR SCORE (FOURTH MOVEMENT, BARS 1–83).

[11]   A mute, on a stringed instrument, is a small clip that fits onto the bridge of the instrument and dampens the vibrations, giving a softer, veiled tone. Brass instruments also may be muted by inserting a conical block into the bell. The instruction *con sordini* in a score means 'with mutes'.

9 SUMMARY

Not all the points listed below will be relevant to every piece of score reading, but you may find these suggestions generally helpful.

1 Before following the music in the score, or even listening to the music, *look* at the score. Note the tempo marking, key and time signatures, textures and *tessituras* so that you have some idea of what to expect. Mark with a highlighter important beat-groupings, rhythmic segments, or even bar lines.

2 Now and again, listen without the score so as to familiarize yourself with the style of the music. Count the pulse carefully while you listen. Then when you turn to the score, *match* your counting immediately the music starts. Once you *are* looking at the score, partly look, partly listen, for confirmation of what you hope you will be hearing.

3 If the tempo is very fast, try following bar lines only to begin with, putting your finger on them if need be.

4 Once you begin to read a score, be aware of dynamic changes, varieties of texture, various *tessituras*, etc., and try to marry these features to the music on the page. Remember: rarely do you read every note!

5 Use a highlighting pen (or pencilled boxes and circles) to mark the places in the score to which your eyes should be directed.

6 Watch out for part crossing (overlapping), especially in chamber music.

7 Follow the most interesting part, but once you are familiar with the music, try following the bass or an inner part, possibly one with plenty of rests. Count carefully in the silent bars!

8 When your score reading is fluent, try to look ahead to what is coming next: usually one (average-length) bar is sufficient. This helps you to anticipate surprises (sudden loud chords, a busy passage of semiquavers, changes of tempo, etc.) and ensures that you do not lose your place.

10 CHECKLIST

As a result of working through this unit:

1 You should be familiar with the workings of the alto and tenor clefs.

2 You should be reasonably happy about the mechanics of score reading in up to five parts, and finding where you are in the score at any given moment.

3 You should be able to keep pace with the music.

4 Finally, your ability to scan a score is also important, as in this way you are taking in two, perhaps three or more staves at one and the same time.

If you are reasonably confident that you are approaching this ideal, then you have completed an excellent week's work.

ACKNOWLEDGEMENTS

Figures 1, 2, 3 and 6   Courtesy of the Mansell Collection.

Figure 4   Courtesy of the National Portrait Gallery, London.

Figure 5   Courtesy of the Royal College of Music, London.

Examples 1 and 2   Courtesy of G. Henle Verlag, München.

Examples 3 and 4   Courtesy of Bärenreiter-Verlag, Kassel.

Video Example 13   Courtesy of Ernst Eulenburg Ltd.

UNIT 15

TWO-STAVE REDUCTION

Prepared for the Course Team by J. Barrie Jones

CONTENTS

DAY 1	1	
	2-2.1	
	2.2	
	2.3	
	2.4	
DAY 2	3-3.1	
	3.2	
	3.3	
DAY 3	4-4.1	
	4.2	
DAY 4	5	
	6-6.1	
DAY 5	7-7.1	
	7.2	
	7.3	

The video items for this unit are on Video-cassette 2.

Audio items can be heard on the Unit 14 audio-cassette, Audio-cassette 6.

Scores needed are Scores 2 and your score of Tchaikovsky's *Serenade for Strings*.

1   CONTENT AND AIMS

The slightly unusual arrangement of exercises and teaching material that you will find here, consisting of a large number of exercises interspersed with relatively little conventional teaching material, and some detailed commentary in the Answers to Exercises section, is a direct result of the remit of this unit, which aims to offer a practical application of your musical common sense to the notational skills you mastered in earlier units. This unit draws essentially on the content of Unit 14. In that unit you worked through scores of increasing complexity, following the various staves while listening to the music. In a sense, Unit 15 reverses this procedure: here, you will practise reducing music for strings (in up to five parts) on to two staves in the form of a keyboard layout. There are a number of exercises for the week, plus several optional exercises if you have time. As you may have guessed, the unit is therefore very much 'do-it-yourself' in character.

You may be wondering what the purposes are of such exercises. If you think about it for a moment, however, you will realize that the ability to reduce a five-stave string score on to a keyboard score tests a remarkable number of skills:

1   You prove – and *im*prove – your reading knowledge of all four clefs (treble, alto, tenor and bass).

2   You have to consider note spacings and part-writing.

3   The layout of the music (part-writing, whether beams and stems go up or down, etc.) has to be clear and legible, and thus notational calligraphy should receive a high priority.

4   With some scores, you gain practice in writing more notes than you would normally expect to find on two staves.

5   With simple scores, the resulting reduction is sometimes playable: for a keyboard player, it is easier to play through such reductions on two staves than to try to play from bigger scores.

6   Where appropriate, you have to remember that one member of the string family transposes: the double bass, whose *actual* notes (i.e. sounding notes) – not those 'on the page' – must be transcribed into your reduction.

7   You can analyse and appreciate the harmonies and harmonic progressions more easily on two (rather than, say, five) staves. All this will help later in the course when you study such matters as stylistic and harmonic analysis, differing kinds of textures, and so on.

8   The process enhances your general ability to read scores, since in the process you find out what is *really* going on in the music in terms of melody, accompaniment, harmonic rhythm and so on.

These skills, as perhaps with others you are acquiring in A214, are unlikely to be attained in one week's study. For this reason, I have provided in Appendix 1 a few further scores for reduction on which you can practise between now and the end of the year. *They are not all to be attempted this week!* Specimen workings for these, which you can compare with your own workings, are provided in Appendix 2.

Because the scores you will work from tend to be full of notes, your reductions will be 'unpianistic' and obviously I am not, in general, expecting you to be able to play them. Here and there, however, there will be cadences and harmonic progressions that you can and should try out at your keyboard. And you should certainly try to play your transcriptions of single lines that were originally in the more unfamiliar clefs, to see whether your written transcriptions are correct.

You will need this week, in addition to this unit: Scores 2 (in Section 5); your score of Tchaikovsky's *Serenade for Strings*; a goodly supply of manuscript paper, pencils and eraser for your exercises; and your keyboard for those areas where you feel it will be useful. There are two video sections. *Note!* Although there is no audio-cassette associated with this unit, you can hear all the relevant extracts on the *Unit 14* audio-cassette (Audio-cassette 6). Certainly it is a good idea to listen to the pieces before working on the related exercises. This is particularly true of those reductions that are unplayable on the keyboard. I shall give the appropriate audio-cassette item numbers as you work through the unit, but please remember that they are for the *Unit 14* audio-cassette.

Apart from the extracts from the Tchaikovsky *Serenade for Strings*, all the extracts you will be reducing are taken from pieces contained in Scores 2. However, in virtually all cases I have reproduced the relevant bars in the text, so it is not essential for you to refer to Scores 2. Where Scores 2 will be useful is when you listen to an item on the audio-cassette. Following the item in Scores 2 should enable you to hear how the few bars you are reducing sound in context. Scores 2 will also be useful when you study the second video section, in Section 5.

In nearly all the exercises there are no *absolutely* right answers, though there can be some wrong ones! With most of the exercises, I shall offer a few hints as to how you should set about your task. (If it helps you, listen to the relevant extract on the audio-cassette. This may be a little difficult in some cases, as many of these examples are quite short.) Attempt your score reduction, then in each case compare your working with mine in the Answers to Exercises section, and study any additional comments I may have made. Then turn back to the appropriate section earlier in the unit, and repeat the whole process. My specimen answers may well be different from yours in detail, but should be the same in principle.

2 SIMPLE REDUCTION

2.1 REDUCTION, ARRANGEMENT AND TRANSCRIPTION

When music is reduced from several staves on to two, the result may be described as reduction, arrangement or transcription. These words are often used indiscriminately, but in this course we shall use them in their strict sense.

Reduction refers to the condensing of music on to two keyboard staves, and not to the omission of any notes present in the original score. This is the meaning the word will have throughout this unit. Every note in the original score must appear in a two-stave reduction. In other words, a reduction is a literal transcription on to two staves. (A harmonic reduction, however, is different and may omit notes.) Similarly, there should be no *additional* notes in a reduction.

However, Bach, Liszt and others often added notes when *arranging* the music of other composers (or themselves) for the keyboard. The essential point about an **arrangement** is that, in using pre-existing material, the arranger does a certain amount of recomposing. Such recomposition may take many forms: shortening, lengthening, reharmonizing, simplifying, adding extra parts, and so on. (Liszt's arrangements are sometimes called **paraphrases**.)

Confusingly, many published arrangements are often described as transcriptions. As I said above, the words are often used loosely. In strict usage, **transcription** means one of the following:

1 a change of notational system (such as doubling or halving all note values for ease of reading);

2 the notating of an unnotated piece;

3 the adapting of a piece for a medium other than the original.

For example, music in an old system of notation may be transcribed into modern notation; or a folk-song (or jazz solo) may be transcribed from a live performance or recording; or a violin piece may be transcribed for a clarinet.

A true transcription, unlike an arrangement, has no creative contribution from the transcriber. This is not to suggest that transcribing is easy or unskilled work.

Having defined our terms, we can now make a start on reduction.

2.2   FROM TWO STAVES TO TWO STAVES

 VIDEO NOTES
UNIT 15, VIDEO SECTION 1

Introduction

The title 'From two staves to two staves' perhaps needs a few words of explanation. The work in this section consists of a reduction from one of Mozart's violin and viola duets, which you studied last week when score reading. The duet is written on two staves, which use the treble clef (violin) and the alto clef (viola). The relevant extract is reproduced opposite as Video Example 1, and you may wish to refer to this extract if you find it hard to read on your screen.

In this video section you will see how I transfer the music on to two staves of the kind normally used for keyboard writing. From time to time you will be asked to stop the video tape and do some work yourself.

There is a Summary of the video section at the end of these notes.

NOW WATCH THE VIDEO SECTION. YOU WILL NEED
MANUSCRIPT PAPER.

During the video section

The first time you are asked to stop the tape, compare Video Examples 1 and 2 printed in the Summary opposite. Notice how every note of the original appears in the reduction.

The second time you are asked to stop the tape, try playing at least bars 5 and 8 of the reduction in Video Example 2.

The third time you are asked to stop the tape, write the appropriate harmonic reduction, in Roman numerals, of bars 5 and 8 of Video Example 2.

There are four chords (not necessarily all different) to go in bar 5, and three in bar 8. Remember that bar 8 is in the key of D major. Check your answer with Video Example 3.

Summary

Video Example 1   Mozart, Duo in G, Rondeau, bars 5–8

Above is Mozart's original for violin and viola. Now here it is, reduced to a keyboard layout:

Video Example 2   Keyboard reduction of Video Example 1

Notice how all the beams and stems are facing in the right direction. Now try to play it if you can, however slowly – one bar at a time, if you like.

Video Example 3 shows a harmonic analysis of bars 5 and 8. Passing notes (which are not part of the harmonic structure) and harmony notes (which are) will be discussed in Unit 17.

Video Example 3   Keyboard reduction with chord symbols for bars 5 and 8

G maj. **Ib   iib   iib   V**   **Ib   V   I** D major

The above harmonic analysis assumes that the harmony notes in the bass occur *on* the beat, not in between. Notice that the C♯ in bar 7 effects a modulation to D, the dominant key, confirmed by a clear perfect cadence in D in the next bar.

2.3   MOZART: DUO IN G

Now let us go back to the first four bars of Mozart's *Rondeau* from his Duo in G, so as to complete the opening phrase. Example 1 gives the first eight bars.

Example 1   Mozart: Duo in G major, K423, Rondeau, bars 1–8

When you reduce this for keyboard, in Exercise 1, the violin will remain unaltered in your right-hand stave (i.e. you copy it exactly), while the viola will have to move from treble to bass clef between bars 4 and 5. Remember the usual rules as to whether stems go up or down, and you should have few problems. Work in pencil (and have an eraser to hand!) for this and all subsequent exercises in this unit. Remember the brace to join the two staves!

 EXAMPLE 1 CAN BE HEARD AS PART OF ITEM 8.

Exercise 1

Now make a reduction of bars 1–4 of Example 1. When you have finished bars 1–4, copy bars 5–8, from Video Example 2, so as to make up the complete 8-bar sentence. Then look at my answer in the Answers to Exercises section.

Throughout this unit, my reductions – and any necessary comments – are given in the Answers to Exercises section. You should turn to this section after completing each reduction so that you can compare your versions with mine; then you should return to the main part of the unit and continue working through it.

2.4   A FEW GENERAL REMINDERS

Remember that you must not add to your reduction extra notes that are not in the original score. Transcribe exactly what is there. This will mean that in most cases this week your reductions will be unpianistic: that is, they will not be playable by two normal-sized hands. Those that are pianistic will be hard to play, however, so in these cases try just a few chord progressions, however slowly. Remember: you are producing not a piano piece (still less a performance of a piano piece), but a version which is easier to read by being written on just two staves, and which avoids unfamiliar clefs. We are not concerned in this course with pianistic versions of complex orchestral pieces, but we do expect to help you to turn scores into 'sound' for yourself. Doing this helps with aural training, helps you to recognize certain harmonic progressions and facilitates the reading and writing of music generally. All these may seem difficult, but don't be at all discouraged. If the layout of your reductions differs from my suggested workings, do not be surprised. Often, more than one acceptable layout is possible; in any case, each exercise will have its own individual problem that is not always readily perceptible until a specimen answer is studied.

3   MOUNT EPHRAIM AND MOZART

3.1   MOUNT EPHRAIM

Now try something a little different. *Mount Ephraim* is a hymn tune, part of which you met in Unit 13. Example 2 is the first phrase of this tune.

As you can see, it appears in string-quartet-style score and thus is on four staves and not two. However, the notes are simple and the short reduction exercise in Exercise 2 will give you a foretaste of what you will be transcribing in Section 6.

Example 2   Mount Ephraim

 PLAY JUST THE TOP LINE OF EXAMPLE 2.

Exercise 2

Make a two-stave reduction of Example 2. In your reduction, arrange the four parts as you would arrange them in a hymn tune. The two upper parts will be in the right-hand stave, and the two lower in the left. The first violin and viola parts will have their stems upwards, and the second violin and cello will have stems downwards. (Note that the bass in bar 3 is slightly different from the one you worked in Unit 13.) Compare your answer with mine in the Answers to Exercises section.

The next exercise asks you to convert your reduction into a keyboard reduction so that notes of equal duration and close enough in pitch to share a stem can do so. In keyboard notation, provided they are not much more than an octave apart, two simultaneously sounding notes on the same stave can happily share a single stem, *provided they have the same duration as each other*. This sort of writing, therefore, is impossible:

Example 3

It must be rewritten thus:

Example 4

Because there are two 'real' parts, each one needs, where appropriate, its own rest. I shall elaborate on this in Section 4.1.

Exercise 3

Now make a keyboard version of your two-stave reduction from Exercise 2. Compare your answer with mine in the Answers to Exercises section.

In nearly all the reductions in the remainder of this unit, you will see that, where practical, I have put notes of equal duration on the same stem, following the convention for keyboard music. Your reductions will not be wrong if you do not follow this convention – provided they are correct in other respects.

3.2   MOZART: DUO IN B FLAT

The next reduction consists of bars 7–10 from the slow introduction to the first movement of Mozart's Duo in B♭, given as Example 5. This music example is taken from a different edition of the work than that used for Example 4 of Unit 14. Note that bar 8, being a long bar, spreads over from one line of music to the next in the version in Example 5. This is known as a **split bar**.

Example 5   Mozart: Duo in B♭ major, K424, Introduction, bars 7–10

EXAMPLE 5 CAN BE HEARD AS PART OF ITEM 9.

In this piece it is sensible to begin the reduction by writing down the notes of smallest value first so as to leave yourself with enough room in the bar for what remains. In fact, because there are so many demisemiquavers here I shall ask you to attempt only bars 9 and 10, though if your writing is fluent, by all means try the whole extract yourself.

In bar 9, the left-hand part could begin as in Example 6.

Example 6

Alternatively, it could begin as in Example 7.

Example 7

But for the second half of the bar, you would have to retain stems up and stems down as in the original, because of the different note values. (See my note on Examples 3 and 4 at the end of Section 3.1.)

> #### Exercise 4
>
> Look carefully at Example 5, then either try bars 9–10 or go straight to my comments in the Answers to Exercises section.

When an extract does not begin at bar 1 (as in Example 5), it is a good idea to include the time signature in square brackets in your reduction. I have not done so in my reductions because the music has to fit within these columns of text, and space is rather limited. You will not have this restriction in your own work.

3.3 'RULES' VERSUS LEGIBILITY

You may well have had some problems in this section, but this is one area where continuing exposure to music of all kinds will improve your reduction skills (and others). In this work, although the notes are the most important

aspect of your reduction, always be sure to include dynamics, phrasings and bowing marks even though the last are not relevant to keyboard writing. (Bowing marks are the slurs between certain pairs of notes.) The placement of stems, beams, phrasing etc. is also important.

In Example 5, whether or not you did all of it yourself, you would probably have got most of the notes right, but the stems and beams might well have pointed the wrong way. Don't worry about this: it takes a very experienced composer to get this right from his or her publisher's point of view! Even then, one publishing house may differ from another in its 'house style'. Just try to remember what you learn about particular situations as you go through these exercises. The best rule to follow is: if the reduction is legible and clear, then it may (officially) be 'wrong', but in practical terms all is well – and you yourself are doing well. If these 'rules' seem somewhat arbitrary or vague, it is rather as I suggested in last week's score-reading exercises: every example is different and each one will pose its own particular problems.

4   FROM THREE STAVES TO TWO

4.1   MOZART: DIVERTIMENTO K563 (1)

And so we proceed one stage further. The two reductions in this section are both extracts from the first movement of Mozart's Divertimento K563. A substantial extract from this movement is given in Scores 2, beginning at p. 44. Our first reduction will be of bars 9–17, reproduced here as Example 8.

 EXAMPLE 8 CAN BE HEARD AS PART OF ITEM 12.

Here, obviously, the problems are greater than the ones you have faced so far. How do you reduce the three stave lines of Mozart's original score into two staves for a keyboard reduction? Generalizations are dangerous because every case is different, but here it seems appropriate to regard the original violin, viola and cello parts as analogous to soprano, alto and bass voices. That being so, it would be reasonable to transcribe this next example generally with two parts (violin and viola) on the upper (treble) stave, with the cello on the lower (bass) stave.

Example 8   Mozart: Divertimento K563, first movement, bars 9–17

Another difficulty with this reduction is identical to the one you encountered when reading the score of the extract in Unit 14: the fact that from bars 9–11 the viola is the highest line on the score. There are a number of points you should bear in mind:

1   If two or three contrapuntal lines occur on a single stave, it is usually best to ensure that the correct rests for each part are placed on the appropriate stave, or area of stave, in the texture. For example, at bar 11, in order to avoid too many leger lines in the bass (lower) stave, the cello as a third part could come up to share the treble stave, as in Example 9; notice the placing of the rests.

Example 9

I admit that in the penultimate sentence 'usually' is not very precise. The placings within the stave for the two minim rests above is frequently found, but not invariably followed. (Often the editor decides what *looks* best: again, clarity takes precedence over 'the rules'.) In theory, when only two parts share a stave, minim and semibreve rests in this context appear thus:

Example 10

When there are three contrapuntal lines sharing the same stave, the same rests would be written thus:

Example 11

Usually, that is! (Notice the extra bit of stave line, the line 'A', for the highest semibreve rest above.)

2   To save clef changes, it is often useful for a high cello line to be placed (temporarily) in the right-hand (treble) stave if there is room. (See Example 9.) Remember in this context that beams and stems will face downwards even if the notes are around the bottom of the stave lines. This preserves the contrapuntal layout of the texture.

3   In scalic passages, look at, and try to take in, groups of four for the purposes of copying out, rather than individual notes.

4   The last beat of bar 10 in the viola part is played as four equal semiquavers: ♫♫, and it is tidier to write out the notes in this way. For now, in bar 13, leave out the notes printed as small type in the top two parts. Both of these notational conventions will be discussed in Unit 17. (There are similar small notes in the next reduction too.)

Exercise 5

Now make a reduction of Example 8. Check your answer with mine in the Answer to Exercises section.

4.2 MOZART: DIVERTIMENTO K563 (2)

Now for the next reduction, we jump ahead to bars 27–33 (Example 12). I have blanked out the bar before the start of the extract.

Example 12 Mozart: Divertimento K563, first movement, bars 27–33

 EXAMPLE 12 CAN BE HEARD AS PART OF ITEM 12.

Exercise 6

Make a reduction of Example 12. Start both left- and right-hand staves with a *treble* clef, and change to bass clef in the left hand just before bar 31. Include the notes in small type, writing them in your reduction exactly as they are in the original. There are two possible layouts for the top two parts: one includes both violin and viola on the right-hand stave, the other uses both staves for these two melodic lines. See which you prefer! Check your answer with mine in the Answers to Exercises section.

You should now break off from this part of the unit in order to study the remaining section of video. The important music examples from the video are reproduced in the following video notes.

5 MORE COMPLEX STRING REDUCTIONS

 **VIDEO NOTES
UNIT 15, VIDEO SECTION 2**

Introduction

This video section aims to give you some further practical hints that will be helpful with the more complex scores in four and five parts.

The pieces we shall be working on are short extracts from the third movement of Handel's Concerto Grosso in B minor, Op. 6 No. 12 (in Scores 2, p. 28), the third movement of Tchaikovsky's *Serenade for Strings*, and the first movement of Schubert's String Quintet in C, Op. 163 (in Scores 2, p. 54). You should have the relevant scores to hand. You will certainly need to have writing materials and manuscript paper to hand, as you watch the video section. You can hear these pieces on the audio-cassette associated with Unit 14 (Audio-cassette 6). They are taken from Items 10 (Handel), 21 (Tchaikovsky) and 18 (Schubert).

There are no instructions to stop the tape during the video section. However, you may wish to stop the tape after each reduction in order to study what has been done. All the reductions that appear on screen are given below in the Summary.

After the video section, you will need to do some harmonic analysis and use your keyboard.

 YOU MAY WISH TO LISTEN TO ITEMS 10, 21 AND 18.

 NOW WATCH THE VIDEO SECTION. YOU WILL NEED THE SCORES MENTIONED ABOVE, AND MANUSCRIPT PAPER.

Summary

The video section starts with the first four bars of the *Variatio* part of the third movement of Handel's Concerto Grosso in B minor, Op. 6 No. 12. Here are the top two parts:

Video Example 4   Handel: Concerto Grosso, Op. 6 No. 12, third movement, extract

And here is the complete reduction, with the cellos and basses added:

Video Example 5   Handel: Concerto Grosso, Op. 6 No. 12, third movement, extract

Remember that a reduction must show the *actual* sounds. These are not necessarily what you see on the page in the original score. Double basses, for example, sound one octave *lower* than written, so their true pitches must be shown in a reduction. Similarly for other transposing instruments, where the written and sounding pitches are not the same (these will be covered in Unit 21).

As a time-saver, the instruction *coll' ottava* (= with the octave) can be added to indicate that the lower octave is added to each individual note. The term *loco* (= in its place) indicates that the single-note notation (i.e. as written on the page) is resumed. You will notice that I do not play the lower octave of bass stave in the video section because the bass of the keyboard does not extend far enough.

You should include any bass figurings in your own reduction; they are useful in any case if you have to check the harmony.

Video Example 6 is the reduction of bars 21–3 of the *Elégie* (third movement) from Tchaikovsky's *Serenade for Strings*.

Video Example 6   Tchaikovsky: Serenade for Strings, *third movement, bars 21–3*

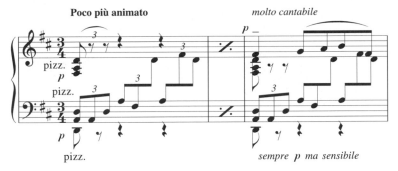

The next example is the first ten bars of Schubert's String Quintet.

Video Example 7   Schubert: String Quintet, first movement, bars 1–10

Video Examples 8 and 9 show alternative reductions for bars 1 to 6.

Video Example 8   Schubert: String Quintet, first movement, bars 1–6

Video Example 9   Schubert: String Quintet, first movement, bars 1–6

Video Example 10 is the complete reduction of the first ten bars, showing a third possibility for bars 1 to 6.

Video Example 10   Schubert's String Quintet, first movement, bars 1–10

After the video

Study the above reduction (Video Example 10) carefully, comparing it with Video Example 7. If you are a pianist, you could try playing the reduction. Certainly you should play the chords in bars 1, 3 and 5.

  TRY PLAYING BARS 1, 3 AND 5.

Finally, some quick harmonic analysis of Video Example 10.

Name the key first, after which you should be able to identify all the chords, using Roman numerals, except the chromatic chords in bars 3 and 9. Leave these for the moment. And the E in bar 8 is a decorative note, so use the second note, the D, as a constituent note of that first chord.

WRITE YOUR HARMONIC ANALYSIS NOW.

Did you get the following?

Bars 1–6:   basically I in C

Bar 7: V^7b–I in C

Bar 8:   iib in C (remember, we're ignoring the E here), then

               Vb in G.

Bars 9–10:   basically I in G major

Play these harmonic reductions yourself, if you can. Remember, they make perfect sense even when played very slowly.

PLAY THE HARMONIC REDUCTIONS.

Video Example 11 below adds these Roman numerals to the score.

Video Example 11   Schubert's String Quintet, first movement, bars 1–10

C major **I**

V⁷b **I** **iib**

G major **Vb** **I**

6 FROM FOUR STAVES TO TWO

6.1 HAYDN: STRING QUARTET, OP. 1 NO. 1

This section includes one further piece of four-stave writing and should, I hope, be one of reasonably manageable proportions. It comes from the Op. 1 No. 1 String Quartet of Haydn. I am going to ask you to attempt to reduce onto two staves bars 11–21 of the second movement, shown in Example 13. As always, remember that your version should be easy to read and should have, as far as possible, an uncluttered layout. Look carefully at Example 13.

 EXAMPLE 13 CAN BE HEARD AS PART OF ITEM 13.

As well as the above preliminaries, try to bear the following points in mind:

1 Change a clef rather than indulge in a riot of leger lines, unless you particularly wish to preserve the elegance of a melodic shape.

2 If pitch permits, allow two melodic lines to have a stave each, rather than putting both on to a single stave with the consequent empty bars above or below. (This may entail a change of clef on one stave giving, for example, treble clefs on both staves.)

3 You should find a workable solution if, in bars 11–12, you reserve the left-hand stave for the cello alone, and in bars 13–15 split the viola's double stops between left- and right-hand staves.

4 Remember that your version may be different from mine and yet be equally valid. If your reduction is clear and legible and the notes are all correct, there is not much more to worry about. If in doubt – and if practicable – see what your tutor has to say.

Example 13   Haydn: String Quartet, Op. 1 No. 1, second movement, bars 11–21

Exercise 7

Now make a reduction of Example 13. Check your answer with mine in the Answers to Exercises section.

7 FROM FIVE STAVES TO TWO

7.1 TCHAIKOVSKY: *SERENADE FOR STRINGS* (1)

And so we come to the last 'teaching' area of this unit. We are concerned here with five-stave systems. (You came across the term 'system', referring to the staves required for one complete 'line' of a score, in Unit 14.) Some five-stave systems can be quite complex and you will find one example in Appendix 1. But much of the Tchaikovsky *Serenade for Strings* is not like this, and I have selected three fairly representative extracts from it to complete your reduction practice for this week. The first extract consists of the opening eight bars of the third movement (Example 14), for which no preliminary hints should be needed.

Example 14 *Tchaikovsky,* Serenade for Strings, *third movement, bars 1–8*

 EXAMPLE 14 CAN BE HEARD AS PART OF ITEM 21.

Exercise 8

Now make a reduction of Example 14. Check your answer with mine in the Answers to Exercises section.

7.2 TCHAIKOVSKY: *SERENADE FOR STRINGS* (2)

Next, a rather trickier extract: bars 53–60 of the waltz movement that precedes the *Elégie*. Example 15 shows the extract. You will see here, in bars 53 and 54, some examples of a tremolo that is both slurred and measured (see Unit 14, footnote 10 for an explanation of tremolo). Alternatively, you could regard these as trills. In bar 54 there is a quintuplet.

 EXAMPLE 15 CAN BE HEARD AS PART OF ITEM 22.

By this stage in the week your study time may be limited, so regard the writing out of this reduction as optional. However, if you do not make a reduction yourself, you should still study my comments and 'solution'. This

is an instance in which the confluence of the inner parts poses a potential problem, so here are two or three suggestions:

1 Keep the cellos on the lower stave with the note stems pointing upwards.

2 The viola double stops should go on the same stave with their stems pointing downwards. Even with the double-bass stems also pointing down you will find that the lower stave is more 'crowded' than usual. Nevertheless, it ought to be legible. Give yourself plenty of space.

3 The tenor clef appears in this exercise: remember that middle C is fixed on the fourth line from the bottom of the stave.

Exercise 9

Now make a reduction of Example 15. Check your answer with mine in the Answers to Exercises section.

Example 15 *Tchaikovsky:* Serenade for Strings, *second movement, bars 53–60*

7.3 TCHAIKOVSKY: *SERENADE FOR STRINGS* (3)

Finally, bars 56–61 from the last movement (Example 16). Again, regard this reduction as optional if you are running out of time. This is easier than the previous one, and therefore I'll leave you to puzzle out the solution.

Example 16   Tchaikovsky: Serenade for Strings, *fourth movement, bars 56–61*

 EXAMPLE 16 CAN BE HEARD AS PART OF ITEM 23.

Exercise 10

Now make a reduction, of Example 16. Check your answer with mine in the Answers to Exercises section.

8   CONCLUSIONS AND CHECKLIST

The only important point here is that score reduction is an exercise where your success rate improves the more frequently you do it. You will almost certainly find that you need considerably more than one week to become fluent in this sort of work. You would perhaps find it useful to work through each of these eight reductions again during the next eight weeks – without referring to this week's efforts – and you will probably be surprised at how much easier the work is the second time round. (You could even try a third time during weeks 24–31!) Apart from consolidating the learning process, this sort of exercise makes a welcome change from the different sort of work you will, in general, be undertaking in those weeks. However, I realize that your study-time is limited, so this suggestion may prove to be impractical.

A checklist of some of the more important suggestions I have made this week may be of help: again I stress that every piece of score reduction you meet will have its own problems – though there will always be a solution – and the following hints cannot claim to be exhaustive in their application.

Try to bear the following points in mind:

1   Cultivate a legible hand.

2   Work in pencil first; you will almost certainly need to re-align the reduction in places, and alter the layout of the note-stems. Ink your work in later, if you have time – and certainly if you are doing a TMA.

3   Every note in the original score must be incorporated into your reduction. Make sure that the correct duration of each note is retained, and that all notes grouped on to a single stem have the same length.

4   Do not introduce extra notes into your reduction.

5   Remember that the double-bass part sounds an octave lower than written in the original.

6   If there is a single line of music on one stave, follow the usual rules for stems and beams.

7   Where there is more than one line of music on a stave, your stems and beams will need to face in whatever direction is necessary for clarity to be preserved.

8   In general, transcribing the shortest-value notes first gives the best layout.

9   Leave a blank stave between your systems should clarity appear to require it.

10 A chord (with one stem) can sometimes be spread out into both staves with advantage, as can a whole melodic or accompanimental line.

11 Double stops that have separate stems in the original can be converted into single-stem two-part writing in your reduction, unless the texture is contrapuntal. In that case, retain the contrapuntal layout of the original score.

12 Be sure to include dynamics, bowing and phrasing.

13 Frequently, more than one textural disposition or layout is possible.

14 In general, avoid empty bars, if you are able – pitch permitting – to spread one or two parts out on to both staves. It looks neater than bars above or below with nothing happening in them.

Appendix 1 is *optional*. It consists of extra exercises for use later in the year. Appendix 2 offers some solutions to Appendix 1.

9   ANSWERS TO EXERCISES

Exercise 1

My reduction is given in Example 17. This is quite pianistic, and you may be able to play it on your keyboard. As I suggested on the video section, play just one bar at a time, however slowly, so as to get the music into your fingers and the musical style into your brain.

Example 17   Mozart: Duo in G major, K423, Rondeau, bars 1–8

Exercise 2

Example 18 gives my reduction. I hope this, at least, did not cause you too much trouble. Check that the viola line is correct in your working.

Example 18   Mount Ephraim

Exercise 3

Example 19 is my version. This is probably the most appropriate keyboard version of Example 18, though you may have something slightly different. (The notes of Examples 18 and 19 are identical, of course!) Note that the four individual phrase marks of the four-stave original reduce to two in both Examples 18 and 19, for reasons of space and common sense – always a factor in this sort of work. You should be able to play Example 19 yourself even if the tempo is rather slow.

Example 19   Mount Ephraim (keyboard version)

Exercise 4

Example 20 is my reduction. The circled numbers refer to my numbered notes below.

You will probably not be able to play this example yourself. Listen to it on the audio-cassette (Item 9), following the reduction.

LISTEN TO ITEM 9.

Example 20   Mozart: Duo in B♭ major, K424, Introduction, bars 7–10

① Above the bracket, between the first ① and the second ①, treble rather than bass clef is perfectly possible.

② In the last three quavers of bar 8 and in the first half of bar 9 I have put the viola's double stops on to single stems. As I wrote in Section 3.2, it is also correct to keep the separate up-and-down stems of Mozart's original for these double stops. In the second half of bar 9, though, there is no

choice. Mozart's original up-and-down stems must be retained because the note values are different in each double-stopped part. The same, of course, is true of the violin part at this point.

③ Notice here that the upward stems in the original violin part face downwards in the reduction, as is the normal practice for notes higher than the middle line of the stave. In double stops such as these, where the note values are the same, it can sometimes make sense for the notes *not* to share stems since, occasionally, different phrasing applies to the two 'lines', even though they are played on a single instrument. This practice is quite common in chamber music, but in orchestral string writing the separation of two notes in this way (individual beams and stems for each) has a different meaning: the section playing that part divides into two (*divisi* is frequently written into the score), each 'half' playing a single line *without* double stopping.

Exercise 5

My reduction of bars 9–17 of the Divertimento movement is given in Example 21.

Example 21   Mozart: Divertimento K563, first movement, bars 9–17

1 In bars 12–14 the violin and viola play the same sort of music at approximately the same pitch range. In this case, their stems are shared in the reduction. As a result, the slurs occur once, not twice. And, as in the present example, the usual practice is for slurs to be *under* the notes if the stems face up, *over* if they face down. Remember that we have omitted the notes in small type in bar 13.

2 Note that in bar 15 of my reduction I have put the rests for the violin part (the crotchet and minim rests) *above* the middle of the stave because there are two contrapuntal parts sharing the same stave here, and we think of the violin as being the upper part – even though it is silent. I explained this idea in Section 4.1 in connection with Example 9. This now creates a problem for the bowing marks in bars 15–17. If I rigidly followed the principle in comment 1 above, these slurs might encroach on the rests. Thus, even though all the stems in the semiquavers of bar 15 face downwards, the slurs go under, not over the stems, so as to avoid the rests in the top part. Similarly with the semiquavers in bars 16 and 17. Other problems should, I hope, be covered in Section 4.1.

This reduction is difficult to play, unless you are a skilled pianist. However, you should certainly try to play the simplified version of bars 9–11 in Example 22, which preserves their harmonic structure.

PLAY EXAMPLE 22.

Example 22

Now, try putting Roman numerals under those chords. (Ignore the third chord of the second bar.)

WRITE IN THE HARMONIES.

You should have:

| IV   viib   I | Vb   V   –   vii | I |

A final question on a point you should always bear in mind in similar musical contexts: did you remember to cancel the F♯ in bar 11 when the cello comes up on to the right-hand stave?

Exercise 6

My reduction of bars 27–33 of the Divertimento movement is given in Example 23. Again, the circled number refers to my numbered comment below.

Example 23   Mozart: Divertimento K563, first movement, bars 27–33

① Some musicians might think it pedantic to include these rests: they are not really necessary, and one finds many genuine piano pieces where, in an analogous situation, they would be omitted. At this stage in your studies, though, it is perhaps better to include them.

A more general point: did you choose to put the cello and violin parts together in the right-hand stave? Since both instruments share the same rhythm, and indeed are playing basically the same melody, this is certainly possible. In this case, you probably have something like Example 24 for bars 27–30.

Example 24

This is fine, though I prefer Example 23 as I find the large gap between the two upper parts makes for difficult reading. Clarity is always an important factor.

Exercise 7

Example 25 is my reduction of the extract from Haydn's Op. 1 No. 1.

Example 25   Haydn: String Quartet, Op. 1 No. 1, second movement, bars 11–21

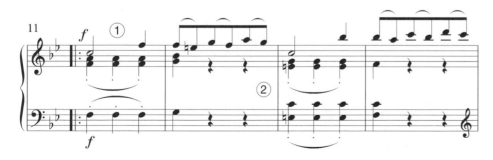

① Here, the stems in the first violin part must go upwards so as to allow room for the second violin and viola on the same stave.

② As I suggested you might, I have split two notes of the viola's double stops between left- and right-hand staves purely to balance the texture out, for appearance's sake. It would not really matter if you kept the original viola part entirely in the left hand.

③ By using two staves here, rather than top stave alone, the high violin part can have its stems facing downwards, which looks much neater.

④ If two instruments play in unison, there is no need to indicate this in your reduction by double-stemming (i.e. giving each note stems on both left- and right-hand sides, one up and one down). Here, your stems might well go down rather than up. However, when in the same stave another part has a downward stem, it looks neater if the higher part's stems face upwards, even though this appears to conflict with the downward stems of the same part in the succeeding bar. Frankly, there is not much to choose between them. Note that the staccato dots in the first violin at 19 and 21 appear above the stave, as you would be unable to see them if they were embedded within it.

⑤ I chose to change clef from treble to bass in this bar to avoid too many leger lines. If you preferred to use more leger lines, rather than break up the smooth appearance of the double octaves by changing clef, this is fine. Either version is acceptable, though possibly neither is absolutely ideal.

Exercise 8

Example 26 is my reduction of the extract from the third movement of Tchaikovsky's *Serenade for Strings*.

Example 26 Tchaikovsky, Serenade for Strings, *third movement, bars 1–8*

① Remember the useful dodge of one stem being shared by two staves, unless the staves – or rather the notes on each of them – are a long way apart. (You would use shared stems only in piano music; do not try it in chorale harmonizations!) You may well have put the three highest parts in bars 1 and 5 entirely in the right-hand stave, which would perhaps be neater than the version in Example 26 but would require a number of leger lines.

② You might have placed the stems upwards in the right-hand part here so as to preserve the general stem direction initiated at the beginning. This would be a good alternative.

③ The part-crossing between second violin and viola should not, of course, be emulated in your reduction: linear simplicity should be your aim.

④ Just a reminder that the unplayability of this chord does not matter in the context of these reductions.

Three final comments: First, with single notes the usual rules regarding the direction of stems tend to apply. With chords, it can be difficult to decide: one looks for the overall 'balance' of up- or down-ness, but one cannot always be certain of a 'right' direction. Secondly, did you remember the double-bass transposition? Thirdly, if the bass part goes low (as here) or the top part is very high, there is a risk of notes from one system encroaching on to a neighbouring system. In such cases, it is a good idea to keep the systems well apart by leaving a blank stave between them.

Exercise 9

My reduction of the extract from the second movement of Tchaikovsky's *Serenade for Strings* is given in Example 27.

Example 27 Tchaikovsky: Serenade for Strings, *second movement, bars 53–60*

① You might have written the first violin part of bars 53–4 an octave lower, with the conventional 8va sign (meaning 'an octave higher'). You met this in Section 3.1 of Unit 14.

② Although the viola and cello parts 'collide' from time to time, the resulting layout is fairly clear, to my mind. At no time is there a problem as to which instrument is playing what.

③ Note the louder dynamic level of the cellos, which in the original medium allows their easily lost sound to come through the texture.

Exercise 10

My reduction of the extract from the fourth movement of Tchaikovsky's, *Serenade for Strings* is given in Example 28.

① In order to preserve the semiquaver value of this double-bass note it must have a separate note (and stem) rather than let it share the cello part. Notice that in this instance we cannot follow the rule of 'note stems together' because the dot belonging to the cello A would then get in the way of the double-bass A.

Example 28 Tchaikovsky: Serenade for Strings, *fourth movement, bars 56–61*

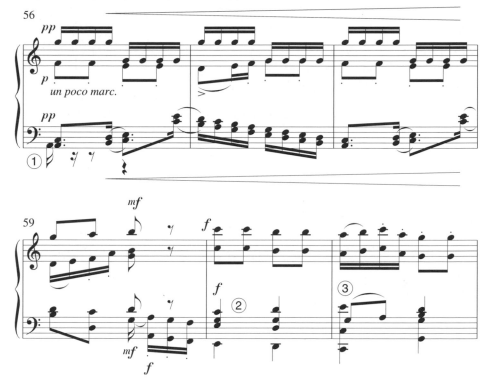

② I put the viola and cello parts on one stem in this bar to save an excessive amount of part-crossing.

③ Here, however, the C on the viola and the high E on the cello share a stem, while the viola G–A keeps its own identity by its separate stems and beams. This preserves the exact note values of all the given parts.

If you are not happy about this, and you have time, try this example once again and see how you get on.

APPENDIX 1

Various (graded) exercises follow in 3, 4 and 5 parts on which you may wish to exercise your continuing expertise during the rest of this year.

The first, Example 29, is bars 144–51 from the fourth movement of Haydn's String Quartet Op. 76 No. 4, 'The Sunrise'. From top to bottom of the system, the instruments are: first violin, second violin, viola, cello.

Example 29 Haydn: String Quartet Op. 76 No. 4, fourth movement, bars 144–51

The second extract, Example 30, is bars 57–68 from the first movement of Mozart's Divertimento K563. From top to bottom of the system, the instruments are: violin, viola, cello.

Example 30 Mozart: Divertimento K563, first movement, bars 57–68

The third extract, Example 31, is bars 50–65 from the fourth movement of Mendelssohn's String Quintet in A, Op. 18. From top to bottom of the system, the instruments are: first violin, second violin, first viola, second viola, cello.

Example 31   Mendelssohn: String Quintet Op. 18, fourth movement, bars 50–65

The fourth extract, Example 32, is bars 1–20 from the fourth movement of Tchaikovsky's *Serenade for Strings*.

Example 32   Tchaikovsky: Serenade for Strings, *fourth movement, bars 1–20*

The fifth extract, Example 33, is bars 70–7 from the third movement of Mendelssohn's String Quintet in B♭, Op. 87. From top to bottom of the system, the instruments are: first violin, second violin, first viola, second viola, cello.

Example 33   Mendelssohn: String Quintet Op. 87, third movement, bars 70–77

70

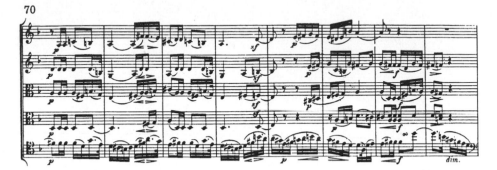

APPENDIX 2

Suggested reductions to scores in Appendix 1 are given below. Until now, all the music you have seen has been professionally produced typeset music, which is typical of the appearance of printed music, but somewhat untypical of musicians' handwriting. In this appendix, all the examples are in manuscript, showing the music as it was actually written. Except for Examples 35(b) and (c), they are all my reductions.

Example 34   Reduction of Example 29 (Haydn: String Quartet Op. 76 No. 4, fourth movement, bars 144–51)

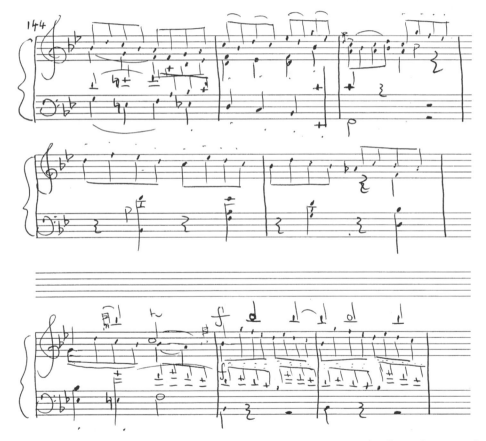

Examples 35(a), 35(b) and 35(c) give three possible solutions to the reduction of Example 30 (Mozart: Divertimento K563, first movement, bars 57–68). They are by J. Barrie Jones, Patricia Howard and David Rowland respectively.

Example 35(a)   Reduction of Example 30 (Mozart: Divertimento K563, first movement, bars 57–68)

Example 35(b)   Reduction of Example 30 (Mozart: Divertimento K563, first movement, bars 57–68)

Example 35(c)   Reduction of Example 30 (Mozart: Divertimento K563, first movement, bars 57–68)

Example 36 Reduction of Example 31 (Mendelssohn: String Quintet Op. 18, fourth movement, bars 50–65)

Example 37 Reduction of Example 32 (Tchaikovsky: Serenade for Strings, fourth movement, bars 1–20)

Example 38 Reduction of Example 33 (Mendelssohn: String Quintet Op. 87, third movement, bars 70–77)

ACKNOWLEDGEMENTS

Grateful acknowledgement is made to the following sources for permission to reproduce material in this publication:

Examples 13, 14, 15, 16, 29 and 32: reproduced by permission of Ernst Eulenburg Ltd, London.

Video Example 1 and Examples 1, 8, 12 and 30: © 1991 Bärenreiter-Verlag, Karl Vötterle GmbH & Co, Kassel, all rights reserved.

Video Example 7 and Examples 31 and 33: reproduced by permission of Dover Publications Inc.

UNIT 16

MOSTLY REVISION

Prepared for the Course Team by Trevor Bray

CONTENTS

DAY 1	1
	2
	2.1-2.2
DAY 2	3
	3.1-3.3
DAY 3	4
	4.1-4.2
DAY 4	5
	5.1
	5.2-5.3
DAY 5	6
	6.1
	7

All the audio-cassette items except one are on Audio-cassette 6. The remaining item – which you will need in Subsection 4.1 – is on Audio-cassette 16.

The video item is on Video-cassette 2.

The scores items are in Scores 1 and in your score of Beethoven's Fifth Symphony.

1 CONTENT AND AIMS

Now that you are roughly half-way through the course, this is an appropriate moment for you to review what you have learnt so far. There have been many skills to acquire – a comprehensive list would cover several pages – but these can be divided basically into three categories:

the skills you need when *looking at* music
those you need when *listening to* music
those you need when *writing* notes on paper.

Within each category, you will often have needed to relate a new skill to one you met previously: frequently the skills are cumulative. Therefore a temporary rest from this evolving process will give you the opportunity to sit back, take a deep breath, and see how the course has developed up to this point. At the same time, you will be able to take encouragement from the fact that you have made real progress during the first half of the course, so that you can then proceed to the second half with renewed interest and enthusiasm.

The first aim of this unit, therefore, is for you to take stock (and take heart!). The second aim, related to the first, is to consolidate the skills you have learnt. I shall give you exercises through which you can test your knowledge of the material from earlier units. These will be self-assessment tests: they will bring to your attention where you have been successful, and will also pinpoint those skills that still need improvement. Time has been allocated for you to deal with the latter, so by the end of the unit you should feel reasonably confident that you have mastered the basic skills taught during the first half of the course.

In order to deal with the three categories of skill you have acquired, the unit is divided into three main parts:

- looking at music (Section 2)
- aural recognition (Sections 3 and 5)
- writing notes on paper (Section 6).

Most of the material in each part will, in some way, help you with your revision. To give some variety, however, Section 4 provides further discussion of melody, a topic first tackled in Unit 4. During this section I shall be discussing some of the ways in which melodies are constructed, and I'll give you working definitions for several features found in melodies. Since much of the material will be breaking new ground, this section will – I hope – provide a welcome change from your continuing revision.

In addition to this unit you will need: your audio-cassette player and Audio-cassettes 6 and 16; Scores 1 and your score of Beethoven's Fifth Symphony; manuscript paper; your video-cassette player and Video-cassette 2.

2 LOOKING

2.1 WORKING WITH TWO STAVES

Let us start by looking at music with two staves.

Exercise

Item 1 on the audio-cassette consists of the hymn-tune, *Capetown* (commonly set to the text, 'Three in One, and One in Three').

 LISTEN NOW TO ITEM 1.

Now refer to Example 1 and answer the questions below:

Example 1 Capetown

(a) How many phrases are there? (Draw in the phrase marks.)

(b) In what key does the extract start?

(c) What is the key at bar 6?

(d) Identify three examples of root-position chords (mark them with the letter a).

(e) Identify two examples of first-inversion chords (mark them with the letter b).

(f) Identify one example of a second-inversion chord (mark it with the letter c).

(g) One of the four cadences is *imperfect*. In which bar does it occur?

(h) Which standard chord progression can be found at the unlabelled square bracket in bar 6? (Mark the chords by writing roman numerals under the stave.)

(i) Identify one example of a dominant seventh (mark it with V^7).

(j) Name the intervals in the melody marked by the brackets x, y and z. (Provide the full description – not merely 'second' or 'fifth', for instance.)

Answers

(a) As you can see from Example 2, there are four phrases. It's not possible to split the music into smaller phrases, since the melody moves on with a steady crotchet pulse through each two-bar 'unit'. Nor is it possible to make only two phrases (bars 1–4 and 5–8), because each of the four phrases closes conveniently with both a longer note and a cadence. (If you need to revise the work you did on phrases, refer back to Unit 4, Section 8.)

(b) The key signature of two sharps provides two possibilities, either D major or B minor. However, B minor can be discounted for three reasons. First, the leading note of B minor is A♯, and there are no A sharps in bars 1–2 (but there are plenty of A naturals!). Secondly, notice the contour of the melody: A–F♯–B–A–G–G–F♯ is more likely to occur in D major than in B minor. (For revision of major scales, see Unit 6, Section 8.) Finally, the first bar opens with a D major chord.

(c) The presence of G sharps in bars 5 and 6 (and no G naturals) points to A major. This is the dominant key; as you may remember from Unit 13 (which dealt with modulation), a major-key piece will usually modulate to its dominant key first. (See Unit 13, Section 2, Guideline 1.)

(d)–(f) There are several examples of root-position and first-inversion chords: see Example 2. The only example of a second inversion occurs at bar 6^1(i.e. the first beat). (Chords and their inversions were discussed in Unit 5, Sections 7 and 8, and in Unit 11. Note that the asterisks in Example 2 mark secondary seventh chords, which will be discussed in Unit 19.)

Example 2   Capetown

a b a b a* a a   a a a b a a a

V⁷

b a b b c a a   a a b* a a

V ⁷   V ⁷

Ic V⁷ I

(g) The second cadence is an imperfect one and it occurs in bar 4; see Example 3. (To revise cadences, see Unit 8.)

Example 3

4   in D major

I V

(h) The unlabelled square bracket marks an example of the Ic–V⁷–I formula. (See Unit 8, Video Section 1 on Video-cassette 1.) Notice that the seventh, D, appears in the alto part on the fourth quaver; this is marked on Example 4.

Example 4

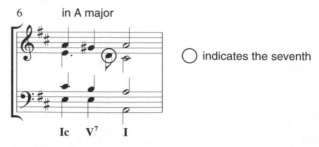

6   in A major

○ indicates the seventh

Ic V⁷   I

(i) The three dominant sevenths in this extract are marked on Example 2. The dominant sevenths in bars 6 and 7 last for only a quaver rather than throughout the chord (the seventh in bar 7 comes on the final quaver – in the tenor part). This is called a passing dominant seventh. In contrast, in bar 2 the seventh lasts throughout the second chord (see the soprano).

(j) Finally, the intervals are:
(x) perfect fourth
(y) minor sixth
(z) minor third.

(Intervals were introduced during Unit 4, Section 7, and discussed further in Unit 6.)

Discussion

If you managed to provide correct answers to most of the questions, you are doing very well. You have gained some basic skills in analysing certain elements in music, and this will be a good foundation for the rest of the course.

On the other hand, if you provided incorrect answers to most of the questions, or could not remember what was required, go back now and make a concentrated effort to revise those areas in which you were deficient. It is essential that you tackle these problems at once because, as you know, the course is basically cumulative. Each new skill learnt depends on a mastery of its predecessor. Therefore, if a link in the chain is missing, further progress will be jeopardized.

So, refer back to those sections which you need to revise, and make a sustained attempt to master them.

DO THIS NOW.

2.2 WORKING WITH FOUR STAVES

Let us move on from working with two staves to working with four. It is obviously more difficult to distinguish which chords are being used when you are reading from four staves, especially when one of these – as in the following example – has the alto (C) clef (in the viola part). You may find it difficult to form a complete picture of all the notes sounding in a chord: you will forget the names of the pitches played by the violins and cello while you painstakingly work out the note on the viola! If you are having difficulty, you can help yourself by transferring all four parts onto two staves, which will both simplify the recognition process and give you practice in transcribing the alto clef. A quicker alternative would be to write on the score the letter-names of the notes in the viola part.

Exercise

Look at the following extract, which is the second of the two minuets from Haydn's String Quartet, Op. 1 No. 1 (1762). Listen to it on the audio-cassette and then answer the questions below.

 LISTEN NOW TO ITEM 2.

1 In which key does the extract start?

2 Which key is reached by bar 12?

3 Describe the eight chords marked (a)–(h); provide full details (for example, tonic chord, first inversion: Ib). Regard the chords in bars 10 and 25 as being in the original key.

With several of the chords you will notice that not all three notes of the triad are present. Therefore the make-up of the chord is *implied* rather than made explicit: you have to make an intelligent guess as to which is the most likely missing note or notes. Two hints: (i) If two notes are missing, the only note given will be the root. (ii) If one note is missing and there is an interval of a third between the two given notes, this usually (but not always) means a root-position chord; if there is an interval of a sixth between the two given notes, this usually suggests a first inversion.

4 Identify by bar numbers two examples of a perfect cadence.

5 Which harmonic formula does Haydn use at the square bracket, bars 25–6?

Example 5 Haydn, String Quartet, Op. 1 No. 1, second minuet

6 Does the second violin sound above the first violin at any point during the second half of the extract (bar 12³ to the end)? If so, provide exact bar references (for example, bar 18³ to bar 19²).

7 During the same section, does the viola sound above the second violin at any point? Once again, provide exact bar references. Although you may well have been able to answer the previous question simply by looking at the score, here you will probably need to transcribe the second violin and viola parts onto a single stave to see exactly what is happening.

Answers

1 The key signature of two flats suggests either B♭ major or G minor. However, the opening notes on the violins, F to B♭ (and on the viola and cello, B♭ to F), suggest – with their alternation of tonic and dominant – B♭ major.

2 The E naturals in the violins at bar 11, resolving up to F, strongly point to F major, the dominant key; and the bass line moves from C (bar 11^3) to F (bar 12^1), dominant to tonic.

3 (a) Although there are only B flats at this point, the tonic chord is implied and is in root position: I.

   (b) Only F and A are present; the chord is most likely to be the dominant in root position: V.

   (c) Submediant, root position: vi. (The D is omitted.)

   (d) Supertonic, first inversion: iib. (The G is omitted.)

   (e) Dominant, first inversion: Vb. (The F is omitted.)

   (f) Tonic, first inversion: Ib. (The F is omitted.)

   (g) Mediant, root position: iii. (The F is omitted.)

   (h) Supertonic, first inversion: iib.

4 The perfect cadences appear at bars 3–4, 7–8, 11–12 and 25–26. See Example 6.

Example 6

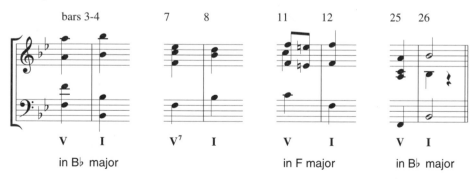

5 The harmonic formula is Ic–V–I. Notice that the bass part drops an octave when the dominant note is repeated. This is a typical pattern, and you will often come across it. See Example 7.

Example 7

(In both Examples 6 and 7 you may have noticed what appear to be consecutive octaves. In fact they are the result of doubling: see Unit 12, Section 5.2.)

6 Yes, the second violin does sound above the first – at bar 14^1 to bar 15^3. Since the second violin imitates the first violin at a bar's distance, the opening octave leap takes the second violin part above the first.

7 From Example 8 you can see that from bar 19^3 to the end of the minuet, the viola part rises above that of the second violin, except for the opening note of bar 22.

Example 8

Regarding question 7: as you become familiar with reading the alto clef, it will become obvious where its part overlaps another. A likely place, for instance, is the passage between bars 22^3 and 24^1, where the high pitches provide more than enough room underneath for a second violin part. Another helpful factor in this minuet is that the viola and cello parts proceed an octave apart from bar 14^3 to bar 22^1, and therefore the pitch of the viola can easily be worked out simply by transposing the cello up an octave. Once you have registered that fact, the process of working out each note of the viola part by 'counting' up or down from the middle line of the stave – a time-consuming, arduous task – is unnecessary.

Indeed it is always helpful when looking at scores to spot where instruments are doubled, because if this is the case you can take one of the doubled parts for granted to a certain extent, and thus reduce the number of things to think about. For instance, at the opening of the minuet the two violins proceed an octave apart – as do the viola and cello when they enter three beats later. Once you recognize that these parts proceed in parallel, this instantly transforms into a simple two-part texture what might appear at first glance to be myriads of notes. Similarly in the next passage, from bar 4^3 to bar 8^1, the two violins are a third apart. Such textures continue more or less throughout the minuet and almost mean that you don't need to work out the viola part at all with reference to the C clef. Only in the last four bars (plus the preceding beat) is this necessary.

Before we leave this exercise, make an effort once again to take time and revise those skills that you have not learnt fully. Time devoted to revision here will undoubtedly pay off later.

DO THIS NOW.

---

3   HEARING: PART I

The second main skill you have been developing in A214 is aural recognition and, as you will have realized, this is a very different skill from discriminating by sight between intervals, chords and suchlike. It requires a different approach: you have to focus sharply so that you are prepared at more or less a moment's notice to identify a chord, or whatever, immediately it has sounded and before it fades away. Most people find aural recognition more difficult than visual recognition, but like any skill it can be improved through practice. A session a week will pay dividends, and if you can get someone to play notes on the keyboard for you to identify, so much the better.

3.1   CHORDS: MAJOR OR MINOR?

Exercise 1

Let us begin by returning to fundamentals and choosing between major and minor chords (see Unit 5, Section 5.3). There are ten examples in Item 3, each played twice. Since both the root and the (perfect) fifth is the same whether a chord is major or minor, the note that makes all the difference is the third: it is, as you know, either major (in a major chord) or minor (in a minor one). So concentrate on that note. Alternatively, familiarize yourself with the expressive feeling generated by each type of chord, and use that as your yard-stick.

You can check that you are on the right track for this exercise by listening to the first two chords (each repeated): the first is major, the second minor. Incidentally, all the chords are in root position but only the first five chords are triads in close position. (The answers are at the back of the unit.)

 LISTEN NOW TO ITEM 3.

When you are listening to music it is important to be able to differentiate more or less instantaneously between major and minor chords. I say this because composers frequently present the listener with either a major or minor chord right at the opening of a piece – even before the melody has entered. When you listen to Item 4, you will find two examples of this: (i) the opening of Beethoven's Third Symphony, the *Eroica* (1803), and (ii) the first few bars of the second movement from Schubert's Piano Trio in E♭ major (1827).

 LISTEN NOW TO ITEM 4.

In each case the composer is obviously saying something fundamental about the music: it is either in a major key (the Beethoven) or minor (the Schubert). However, occasionally the composer hedges his or her bets. Only the root and (perfect) fifth are sounded, leaving the listener uncertain as to whether the key is major or minor. A good example of this comes at the beginning of Beethoven's Ninth Symphony, the 'Choral' (1822–4). Only two pitches arc sounded, an A and E. Is the key A major or A minor? After roughly 30 seconds, Beethoven provides the answer. Neither! He switches to a D minor arpeggio. This settles which mode it is, but our expectations are reoriented. The A–E interval didn't imply the tonic chord but the dominant! (The C♯ was omitted.) You can hear this in Item 5.

 LISTEN NOW TO ITEM 5.

Occasionally, too, a composer can make a statement saying something like: 'I want to set up a conflict between the major and minor at the very outset of my piece so that it starts at a moment of high tension and drama. Right at the beginning you'll be knocked sideways.' Schubert does this at the opening of his String Quartet in G major (1826), as you can hear in Item 6. A chord of G major, beginning *piano* but immediately growing louder, is cut short and replaced by a G minor chord, played *fortissimo*.

 LISTEN NOW TO ITEM 6.

Schubert retains the same tonic for both chords. However, an even greater dramatic effect can be achieved by keeping the idea of juxtaposing major and minor chords but *changing* the tonic. Vaughan Williams adopts this procedure in his First Symphony, *A Sea Symphony* (1903–9), for soloists, chorus and orchestra, and by doing this he creates one of *the* great openings in musical literature. As you can hear in Item 7, a short trumpet fanfare on a B♭

Figure 1   Ralph Vaughan Williams (1872–1958), in a pencil and chalk portrait by Joyce Finzi, dated 1947.

minor chord is repeated in part by the chorus to the words, 'Behold, the...'. For a split second one wonders, 'Behold the what?' The text is completed with 'Behold the sea itself' and, for the word 'sea', Vaughan Williams switches to a D major chord – a master-stroke that is tremendously effective at creating the sense of astonishment and wonder as the sea is revealed.

 LISTEN NOW TO ITEM 7.

From these examples, you will realize how useful it is to be able to recognize promptly whether a chord is major or minor. So if you had difficulty with the above exercise, try it again. (I hope you will have forgotten the answers by now!)

3.2 MELODIES: MAJOR OR MINOR?

Not only is it important to distinguish between major and minor chords, you also need to be able to tell whether a melody is written in a major or minor key. If you play or hum through a melody in the major and then alter the relevant notes to turn it into the minor, you will hear how the minor version has a very different character. Whether a melody is major or minor is thus an important part of its make-up – sometimes, indeed, the most important part.

Exercise 2

When you listen to Item 8, you will hear eight melodies, some major, some minor. Which are which? (The answers are at the back of the unit.) The melodies are taken from the following:

1 Beethoven, Fifth Symphony, Trio from the Scherzo.

2 Purcell, *Dido and Aeneas*, Dido's Lament.

3 Tchaikovsky, *Serenade for Strings*, Waltz.

4 Mozart, *The Marriage of Figaro* (*Le Nozze di Figaro*), 'Si vuol ballare'.

5 Mozart, Symphony No. 40, opening.

6 Schubert, Eighth Symphony (the 'Unfinished'), first movement, second subject.

7 Wagner, *Die Walküre* (The Valkyrie), Act III, scene (i), 'The Ride of the Valkyries'.

8 Elgar, *Enigma Variations*, theme.

 LISTEN NOW TO ITEM 8.

Discussion

The last example might have confused you slightly because of its last note. Except for this, everything fitted nicely into the minor. So what is Elgar doing? When you listen to the whole of his theme (in its proper orchestral setting) as Item 9, you will be able to answer that question for yourself. Think about whether the music is minor or major, and what happens on the very last note.

 LISTEN NOW TO ITEM 9.

Answer

Elgar's theme is in three parts. The first part is in the minor, then comes a shorter section in the major before a return to the minor for the third part. (You will have noticed that the theme of the first part returns for the third part too, although now joined by a counter-melody on the cellos. This provides a short and simple ternary scheme.) Finally, for the very last note, the music changes to the major once again.

Discussion

This last feature is called a ***Tierce de Picardie*** (Picardy third). In a *Tierce de Picardie,* a predominantly – or, more often, wholly – minor melody ends with the major instead of minor third. You can hear an example at the end of the Coventry Carol in Item 10.

 LISTEN NOW TO ITEM 10.

3.3 INTERVALS

If we now look at the first part of Elgar's *Enigma Variations* theme, we see that two intervals play an important part in defining its shape while at the same time providing it with a particular character.

Example 9   Elgar, Enigma Variations, *first part of the theme*

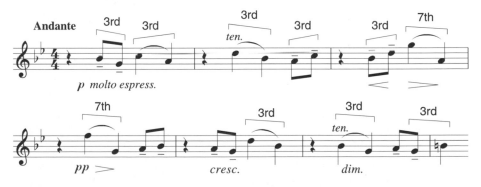

These intervals are the third and the seventh. As we shall see in Section 4, a composer may well focus on a particular interval when writing a melody. If this principle were applied rigidly, it would create too mechanical an effect, but Elgar avoids the mechanical by contrasting falling and rising thirds, and by introducing two falling sevenths half-way through this part of his melody. The gentle oscillation of thirds is interrupted by two strong descending leaps, arching down from the highest notes in the melody – a contrast that ensures that our attention does not wander.

Exercise

I shall shortly ask you to listen to the extracts in Item 11 and identify which interval is of primary importance in each one. This will not be easy, because you will be dealing with 'real music', and several of the examples are in a fast tempo. So I would like you to prepare yourself by referring back to two of the exercises you attempted earlier in the course where you were asked to identify intervals aurally – as Audio-cassette 2 Item 8 (associated with Unit 4) and Audio-cassette 3 Item 18 (Unit 6). There the intervals were isolated, leaving plenty of time for you to make your choice, so the task was considerably easier.

NOW TRY THESE EXERCISES AGAIN.

Exercise 3

Having 'resharpened' your ears, you can now tackle the more difficult exercise. Your task is to listen to the seven extracts in Item 11 and, for each one, identify which interval is of primary importance. To get to grips with an extract, listen to it and try to memorize it. Then you will be able to hum the melody to yourself, slowing it down so that you can think about which intervals are being used and which is the predominant one. Take your time. Do not worry whether the predominant interval is major or minor, or whatever, only whether it is a third or fourth, and so on (the answers are at the back of the unit). The following points might help you with the more complex extracts:

> With Extract 3, the opening interval of the melody – repeated several times – is the predominant one. (The melody begins on the third beat of the second bar.)

> With Extract 4, the most important interval can be heard twice on the first four notes of the violin.

In Extract 6, there are two predominant intervals – listen only to the *first* and *third* phrases.

In Extract 7, there are again two intervals.

 LISTEN NOW TO ITEM 11.

In the following paragraphs I deal with each extract in turn.

EXTRACT 1

Here, the introduction to the scherzo of Beethoven's Ninth Symphony begins with four triple-hammerblows that outline a falling octave. The first three are clearly separated from each other by intervening rests, so that the listener has sufficient time to register exactly what the interval is.

Example 10   Beethoven, Symphony No. 9, scherzo

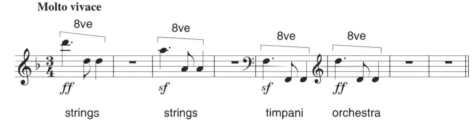

When the main part of the scherzo begins, it becomes clear why Beethoven has singled out this interval for such emphatic treatment. It becomes the opening idea of a theme that he then introduces on different instruments, one by one. Because he has planted the falling-octave shape firmly in the listener's mind, it is so much easier to hear the different entries as the melody comes in – firstly, on the second violins, then on the violas, then on the cellos, then on the first violins and, finally, on the double-basses. It is nevertheless quite difficult to hear, but have a go.

 LISTEN NOW TO ITEM 12.

EXTRACT 2

This example, the opening of the first movement of Beethoven's Fifth Symphony (1807–8), is similar to the example above. Beethoven provides the listener with ample opportunity to identify the interval, both by repeating it and by separating each occurrence with rests. Once the interval (a third) has been established, the musical argument can get under way without further ado (as you can discover by playing the first minute or so of your recording on Side 2 of Audio-cassette 16).

EXTRACT 3

The rising sixths in this extract from the aria 'Libiamo ne' lieti calici' ('Let's drink from the joyous chalices'), from Act I of Verdi's *La Traviata* of 1853, provide the opening of the melody with a strong, positive shape suitable for a drinking song.

EXTRACT 4

This unambiguous opening of Haydn's String Quartet, Op. 76 No. 2 (1797), made such an impression on its contemporary listeners that the quartet was nicknamed 'The Fifths'. The opening motif on the first violin, shown in Example 11, is used to generate much of the material that follows.

Example 11   Haydn, String Quartet, Op. 76 No. 2, opening

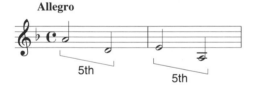

EXTRACT 5

One of Beethoven's greatest melodies, the main theme from the finale of his Ninth Symphony, is constructed almost entirely from seconds. Only in two of the six phrases – the third phrase and the fifth – are other intervals introduced to provide variety. (You played this melody in Section 12.1 of Unit 4.)

Example 12   Beethoven, Symphony No. 9, finale, main theme

EXTRACT 6

For the opening theme of his G minor symphony (K550, 1788) Mozart balances a small interval, a second (falling), with a larger one, a sixth (rising) – just as Elgar did in his theme for the *Enigma Variations*.

Example 13   Mozart, G minor Symphony, K550, opening theme

EXTRACT 7

And finally, Brahms, at the opening of his Fourth Symphony (1885), alternates falling thirds and rising sixths:

Example 14   Brahms, Symphony No. 4, opening

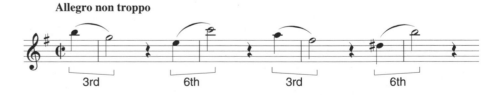

Notice that if we transpose some of the pitches of this theme down an octave, we find a rigid pattern of descending thirds as shown in Example 15.

Example 15

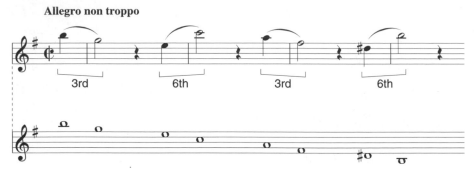

And, moreover, the next four bars of the theme are derived from a constant pattern of ascending thirds:

Example 16

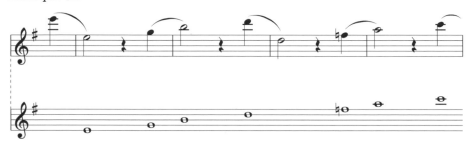

But Brahms avoided such mechanical effects by a judicious choice of octave transpositions both up and down for certain of the pitches. The 'skeleton' provides the theme with a very strong framework, but some variety had to be introduced to dispel a feeling of monotony. To get a sense of this, listen to the complete opening theme.

LISTEN NOW TO ITEM 13.

The exercise on Item 11 was tough, and you may well have had difficulty in identifying the primary interval(s) in the extracts. The sixths are particularly hard to spot, so don't worry if these eluded you at your first attempt. However, notice that in each extract, the most important interval or intervals in a tune have been placed at the beginning. Composers do this so that the listener doesn't miss this crucial information. If this information were delayed, there would be room for confusion or ambiguity. (Mind you, a composer may wish at times to provoke such a response.) So listen once more to the extracts, following the music examples where necessary, and concentrate on the opening interval(s).

DO THIS NOW.

4 MELODY

So far in this unit, the emphasis has been on revision: the aim of the exercises has been to reactivate and strengthen skills you have already learnt. In Section 4, however, you will be breaking new ground once more. Melody, first introduced as a topic in Unit 4, will be discussed further, and this should act as a temporary respite from revision – which, though no doubt beneficial, can become tedious!

4.1 MOTIF

We have just seen how a pattern is produced in a melody when a composer concentrates on a certain interval. Patterns can be created with the other elements too. Consider, for instance, Brahms's treatment of *rhythm* in the opening theme from his Fourth Symphony. The initial rhythm

is repeated throughout the first eight bars:

Example 17   Brahms, Symphony No. 4, opening theme

It so happens with this example that the repetitions of this rhythm coincide with the repetitions of the interval, but this need not be the case (as we shall see below). None the less, such synchronization provides us with a good example of a **motive** or **motif**, a short musical idea that has a distinctive rhythmic and melodic shape, and that can be used to build up a substantial section of music – or even a whole movement or complete piece. Composers differ in how strictly they deploy their motifs. Some saturate their music with them; others prefer a more relaxed treatment. In addition, composers often vary their approach between different works or different movements.

One of the most influential examples of 'motivic saturation' can be heard in the first movement of Beethoven's Fifth Symphony. We have noted already how the (descending) third plays a prominent role during the opening few bars of the movement, as indeed it does subsequently. Notice, though, that Beethoven does not restrict himself to using only a third; seconds and fourths appear as well, as you can see in Example 18.

Example 18   Beethoven, Symphony No. 5, first movement

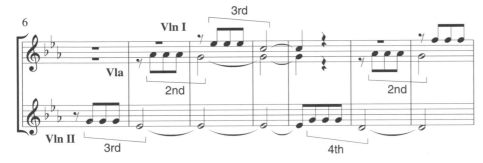

Thus Beethoven's motif is not primarily defined by its intervallic quality – or even, we might think, by its melodic shape. Rather it is its rhythm that is most important, and even a brief glance at the first three pages of the score will make it obvious how Beethoven relentlessly repeats the rhythmic pattern of his motif

even though the melodic shape is sometimes altered from descending to ascending, as in Example 19.

Example 19

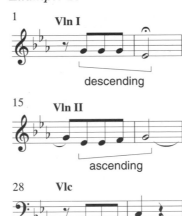

 LOOK NOW AT THE SCORE.

If you now turn to bar 59, you will see the movement's second theme, which appears in the horns. ('Cor.' in the left-hand margin is short for *corni*, the Italian for horns. See Unit 9, Section 4.1, for the abbreviations of other instruments.) Even here the new theme begins with the

rhythm (bars 59–60).

Exercise

My question to you is this: during bars 59–94, are there further appearances of the motif? If so, on which instruments? ('Vc.' is short for *Violoncello*, and 'Cb.' for *Contrabasso*, the Italian for double bass.) Don't forget that the motif is easy to distinguish by its initial three quavers, even though the final note varies – being sometimes a crotchet and sometimes a minim. Note also that it is the stringed instruments that take up roughly the lower half of each system.

Answer

Yes. During roughly the first half of this section, the motif can be heard on the cellos and double basses (at bars 65–6, 69–70, etc.), and during the second half on the violas and double basses (bars 84–5, 86–7, etc.).

Discussion

Since many of the instruments are playing minims and crotchets, the three-quaver rhythm stands out visually, most clearly perhaps in the bottom line of each system.

When you listen to the opening of Beethoven's first movement up to bar 94, concentrate on the various appearances of the motif. The symphony is on Side 2 of Audio-cassette 16.

 LISTEN NOW TO THE OPENING OF THE FIRST MOVEMENT.

Notice that, as in the music up to bar 59, the motif's interval varies. The original third becomes a fourth or fifth. In other words, the interval has been *expanded*. Sometimes composers use this process when creating themes: an interval is expanded at each subsequent appearance to generate part of a theme. Examples 20 and 21, which you can hear as Item 14, give instances of this.

Example 20   Schubert, Die Zauberharfe (The Magic Harp), *overture*

Example 21   Elgar, Symphony No. 2, finale

 LISTEN NOW TO ITEM 14.

In each case, the interval becomes larger and larger. In the first movement of Beethoven's Fifth Symphony, we have seen him use the opposite process, *contraction*. The original interval of a third became a second (see bars 7–8, violas).

Vertical expansion of the type illustrated in Examples 20 and 21 is straightforward to hear, since the implacable repetition of the rhythm compensates for the disorientation caused by the ever-widening interval. Motivic expansion can take place on a *horizontal* plane too. In the following example – the opening of the finale of Beethoven's Piano Sonata, Op. 10 No. 1 (1797) – the vertical expansion of the opening motif gives way to its horizontal expansion, the original one-bar motif being lengthened to two bars. Again, this type of modification is clearly audible.

 LISTEN NOW TO ITEM 15.

Example 22   Beethoven, Piano Sonata Op. 10 No. 1, finale, opening

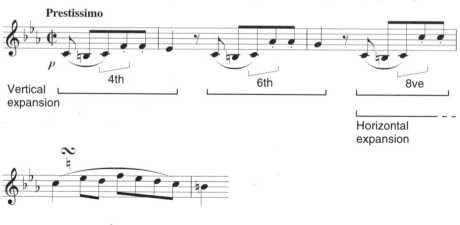

Modification can also take place in the form of **decoration**, and as long as the motif or theme has been presented clearly at its first appearance, then the ear accepts the new material as decoration rather than a new element. You can hear this in the Mozart and Chopin extracts in Item 16.

Example 23   Mozart, Symphony No. 35 ('Haffner'), K385, finale

Original version of motif   Decoration

Example 24   Chopin, Nocturne in E♭ major, Op. 9 No. 2

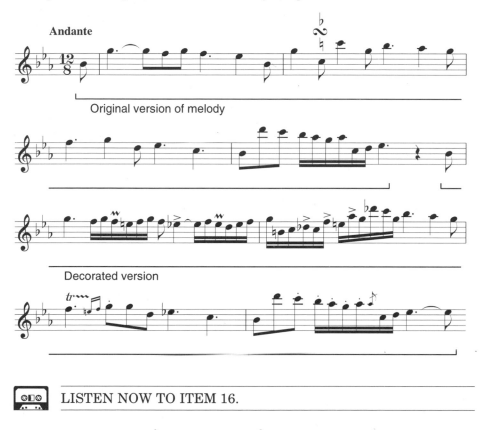

Original version of melody

Decorated version

 LISTEN NOW TO ITEM 16.

4.2   SOME DEFINITIONS

We have seen that a **motif** is a short musical idea with a distinctive rhythmic and melodic shape, and that it can be used as a building block in the construction of a piece (see also Unit 4, Section 11.4). A particularly short motif, say of two or three notes, is sometimes called a **cell**.

A more extended musical idea is often called a **motto**: this usually appears at the opening of a composition and then reappears at decisive moments as the work unfolds. An example can be heard at the outset of Tchaikovsky's Fourth Symphony (1878). There is a fanfare, which is repeated subsequently at important points during the first movement and once again in the finale. If you listen to this motto on Item 17, you will hear that it is longer than a motif, and itself contains repetitions of motifs.

LISTEN NOW TO ITEM 17.

A short musical idea similar to a motif is a **figure**. Like a motif, this can be used to build up a section of music, but it has a less distinct character and so may be harder to remember. The first prelude from Book I of Bach's *The Well-tempered Clavier* (*Das Wohltemperierte Clavier*; 1722) contains a typical example, as shown in Example 25.

Example 25   Bach, The Well-tempered Clavier, *Book I, first prelude*

When you listen to this, you will realize that the music consists very simply of a continuous flow of semiquavers, and therefore – except for its arpeggio shape – there is little to differentiate this pattern from another series of semiquavers. For this pattern to be called a motif, it would need a much more distinct rhythmic shape.

 LISTEN NOW TO ITEM 18.

The straightforward arpeggio figure continues unchanged almost throughout Bach's prelude. You will see something rather different, however, if you turn to page 11 of Scores 1 and look at the closing bars of Corelli's Concerto Grosso, Op. 6 No. 4 (from bar 91b onwards). You can see Corelli using a range of figures, each lasting for a few bars before the next is introduced: look at the violin parts.

Often figures are used for an accompaniment – to a song for instance. Their neutral character does not distract the listener away from the importance of the melody.

The terms 'theme' and 'melody' have been mentioned countless times already. A **theme**, you may well have noticed, often consists of several repetitions of one or more motifs, and is not always complete in itself (see Unit 4, Section 11.4). None the less, it will be a major component of a piece and will be repeated in a recognizable form several times, alternating with different material. The two following examples, by Mozart (Symphony No. 41) and Beethoven (Piano Sonata, Op.2 No. 1), are each constructed basically out of two motifs, which we'll call (a) and (b). As you listen to these themes, notice that whereas the Mozart example can be considered (just about) to be complete, the Beethoven example cannot (since it ends on a dominant chord).

 LISTEN NOW TO ITEM 19.

Example 26   Mozart, Symphony No. 41 ('Jupiter'), K551, opening

Example 27   Beethoven, Piano Sonata, Op. 2 No. 1, opening

Sometimes it is appropriate to use the term **subject** instead of **theme**. We might, for instance, refer to the theme of a fugue as its subject. (You will be introduced to fugue in Unit 30.) In sonata form, too, the different themes can be called **first** and **second subjects** (or, indeed, first and second groups: see Unit 10, Section 7). A **melody**, unlike a theme, is usually complete, either self-standing or forming part of a piece. It is, as its name suggests, more melodious in nature, and therefore suitable for singing, humming or whistling. Here is a well-known melody by Schubert taken from his song, *Du bist die Ruh* (You are my rest). You have already heard this song performed in Television Programme 2; a translation of the words is given in the notes for this programme.

Example 28   Schubert, Du bist die Ruh

voll Lust und Schmerz zur Woh - nung hier _____

mein Aug und Herz, _____ mein Aug und Herz. _____

This melody is constructed in a similar way to the Mozart and Beethoven themes above – by repeating several motifs. With the Schubert melody the motifs are a, b and c, with variants a′ and c′. Yet the smoothness and relatively restricted range of the vocal line make it more melodious than the Mozart and Beethoven themes. To remind yourself of Schubert's melody, listen to the first verse on Item 20.

 LISTEN NOW TO ITEM 20.

A word of caution: the line dividing melodies from themes is not clear-cut, and moreover the terms are often used synonymously. So don't worry too much about distinguishing one from the other. And by the way, **tune** is a less formal way of referring to melody.

Exercise 4

Consider the following extracts, and for each one decide whether it is a motif, figure or theme. (The answers are at the back.)

Example 29   Handel, Zadok the Priest

Example 30   Mozart, Sonata in B♭, K333, opening

Example 31   Mendelssohn, Symphony No. 4, opening

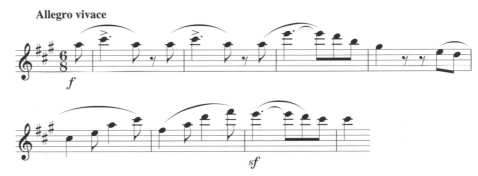

Example 32   Bruckner, Symphony No. 5, finale

Example 33   Fauré, Chanson d'Amour

We have seen that when you are analysing a theme or melody, you need to consider how the motifs fit together (for example, motif a is followed by motif b; then comes motif a again, then b). But there may be other features related to the use of motifs – for example, **sequence**. A sequence is produced when a short section of the theme is repeated (not necessarily exactly), beginning on either a higher note, a **rising sequence**, or a lower one, a **falling sequence**. This example of a rising sequence followed by another comes from the Corelli concerto referred to earlier:

Example 34   Corelli, Concerto Grosso, Op. 6 No. 4

The first series of sequences (bars 1–6) consists of two-bar 'units' and is **modulating**; the second series (bars 8–11) consists of one-bar 'units' and is **diatonic** (that is, the key does not change for the repetitions). If you consult your Corelli score (Scores 1, at the top of page 8), you will be able to verify this point since, with the first series of sequences, the initial unit is in G major, the second unit is in A major and the third is in B minor. On the other hand the second series of sequences does not stray from D major. Note also that with the first sequence, not only is the theme sequential but so are all the other parts in the score. The whole texture is being moved bodily upward a tone at a time. Thus you can have a sequence in any part of the texture.

LOOK NOW AT SCORES 1.

One final point to remember about sequences is that the repetition is immediate: no new material can be introduced between each unit of the sequence. If it were, you would be dealing with a repeated motif or figure, not a sequence.

Our brief discussion of sequences brings this section on melody to a close. There are yet further features associated with melody – such as inversion, augmentation and diminution – but these will be introduced later in the course. For now, though, pause and review the material you have studied here on melody. While not taxing in nature, the discussion has included working definitions of at least twenty terms (although admittedly not all these were new), and it would be prudent before going on to run through these terms in your mind, ensuring that you know what they mean and can provide examples.

DO THIS NOW.

5   HEARING: PART II

5.1   RHYTHM

After that excursion into melody, we return to revision of aural skills. So far, you have listened to features of music that relate to pitch, and dealt with these questions:

1   Are the chords or melodies in the major or the minor?

2   What are the intervals?

Now we shall proceed to rhythm – a topic that was introduced, you'll remember, as early as Unit 1.

As we saw in the previous section, the rhythmic element in a motif is very important. A composer can concentrate on this element, treating the melodic element as subsidiary to a certain extent. That is what Beethoven does in the first movement of his Fifth Symphony, and there is a similar example in the scherzo of the same symphony.

Exercise 5

Your task here is to write down the rhythm of the scherzo's main theme. To do this you will need to listen several times to Item 21, and try to memorize it. Then write down its rhythm.

Try to decide straight away whether it is in $\frac{2}{4}$, $\frac{3}{4}$ or $\frac{4}{4}$, and don't worry about the pitches; only the rhythm is wanted. Remember that the beat is fast in this movement. (The answer for this exercise is at the back of the unit.)

If you need guidance about distinguishing $\frac{2}{4}$, $\frac{3}{4}$ or $\frac{4}{4}$, refer to Unit 1, Section 3.

 LISTEN NOW TO ITEM 21.

Discussion

The rhythm is very repetitive; the rhythmic motif

continues throughout the extract you heard. Notice that this rhythm sounds similar to that in the first movement. The motifs in the two movements are notated differently:

third movement   first movement

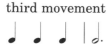

and have different stress patterns:

third movement   first movement

but at their differing tempi they create an aurally similar effect. Because of this, the two movements relate to one another – the scherzo being based rhythmically on the opening movement. This gives a feeling of unity to the symphony.

In the following exercise there are some more rhythms to notate. Always try to memorize the extracts in question as quickly as possible before writing them down. This not only strengthens your musical memory; it means that you don't have to keep repeating the extracts on the cassette!

It is also helpful to decide on the time signature as early as possible since this provides you with some sort of orientation. Even a wrong choice can speed up the process, because you'll soon realize that you *have* made a wrong choice, and you can eliminate it as a possibility.

Exercise 6

There are six extracts in Item 22. They are in $\frac{2}{4}$, $\frac{3}{4}$ or $\frac{4}{4}$, and one begins with an anacrusis. Listen to the extracts and notate their rhythms. The first extract opens with a chord held for two bars before the melody enters, and the third extract a bar of an accompaniment figure. Listen out, too, for the occasional grace note (acciaccatura) in Extracts 3 and 6. Remember that it is only the rhythm of the melody that you are concerned with. (The answers for this exercise are at the back.)

 LISTEN NOW TO ITEM 22.

Discussion

In all those extracts, repetition is an important part of their rhythmic structure. Either short rhythmic motifs are repeated – the third example (Verdi) consists of three-and-a-half repetitions of the same idea – or the second half of the example repeats the first half.

Composers repeat rhythmic elements to make the theme more memorable, of course, but also to provide unity – ensuring that the music fits together. It is difficult to think of a theme that lacks repeated rhythmic elements in its structure.

5.2 CADENCES IN THE MAJOR

Finally, to conclude the aural component in this unit, let us turn our attention to cadences. In Unit 8 you were introduced to the four types of cadence:

perfect	imperfect	plagal	interrupted
V–I	I–V	IV–I	V–vi
	or		
	[other chord]–V		

and in Section 7.2 of Unit 8 you identified, aurally, examples of each type. Here is a similar exercise to help you revise.

Exercise 7

Item 23 contains four extracts from the first half of the slow movement of Haydn's Keyboard Sonata in C (1773). Each extract ends with a cadence: what are the cadences? You will probably have to listen to each extract several times before you can spot them. Incidentally the third and fourth cadences are in the dominant key, C major (the slow movement being in F major). (The answers for this exercise are at the back of the unit.)

 LISTEN NOW TO ITEM 23.

Identifying cadences *in situ* is obviously more difficult than identifying them when they are played as isolated examples. Here, in the context of Haydn's sonata, the complex keyboard figuration may well have been off-putting. However, as always with cadences, you have to concentrate either on the bottom line (to work out which two chords are being used) or on the particular expressive effect of the pair of chords heard (or use both methods in combination). Other elements in the music – such as changes of texture or of tessitura (see Unit 14, Section 3.4) – have to be ignored.

Of the four cadences, I expect you found the second the most straightforward. If you look at Example 35, which shows the first half of the slow movement, you'll see that the harmony here (marked with the 2) was basically V^7–I in F major, a clear perfect cadence.

Cadence 4 was also perfect, but now in C major; and note that Haydn included at this point the formula Ic–V^7–I with the octave drop in the bass between Ic and V^7, as you can see in Example 36.

Example 35 Haydn, Keyboard Sonata in C, slow movement

Example 36

In C major   **Ic**   **V⁷**   **I**

Cadence 3 was of exactly the same type as cadence 4 but, to confuse you, the resolution onto the tonic chord skipped up an octave or so in the right hand and disappeared completely for a beat in the left! See Example 37:

Example 37

In C major   **Ic**   **V⁷**   **I**

The only cadence that was not perfect was the interrupted one at the end of the first extract, and it is perhaps worth noting here that the interrupted cadence in a major key (but not a minor key – see below) has a distinctive feature that none of the other cadences has. That is, it ends on a *minor* chord. In a major key the three other cadences (perfect, imperfect and plagal) all end on a major chord. So if you can distinguish between major and minor chords with confidence, you need never again wrongly identify an interrupted cadence in a major key! To consolidate your work on the cadences in the Haydn piece, it will be helpful to listen to the first half of Haydn's movement complete.

 LISTEN NOW TO ITEM 24.

5.3   CADENCES IN THE MINOR

To follow our exercise with cadences in a major key, here is one for cadences in the minor. If you have difficulty with identifying cadences in the minor, the following guideline could help:

- **In a minor key each of the cadences consists of a unique arrangement of major and/or minor chords.**

Thus we get:

perfect cadence	=	major (V)	→ minor (i)
imperfect cadence	=	minor (i or iv)	→ major (V)
plagal cadence	=	minor (iv)	→ minor (i)
interrupted cadence	=	major (V)	→ major (VI)

For the cadence-spotter, therefore, the situation here is even more advantageous than in a major key. Whereas in a major key only one cadence (the interrupted) has a unique combination of major and minor chords, in the minor key *all four* cadences have a unique arrangement. Once again, success is guaranteed if you can distinguish correctly between major and minor chords.

Exercise 8

We are going to look at some more cadences – in the Sarabande from Handel's Keyboard Suite in D minor (1739). The cassette item is divided into four sections, with pauses in between. Which cadence comes at the end of each section? (The answers are at the back.)

 LISTEN NOW TO ITEM 25.

Discussion

If you look at Example 38, you can see the three perfect cadences at bars 3–4 (in D minor), 15–16 (in A minor) and 23–24 (D minor again). The only cadence that is not perfect is the imperfect one at bars 7–8. Notice that the first chord in this cadence is not the tonic chord but the subdominant in first inversion, ivb. None the less the cadence ends with the dominant chord, and the feeling of incompleteness associated with an imperfect cadence is still there.

Example 38   Handel, Keyboard Suite in D minor, Sarabande

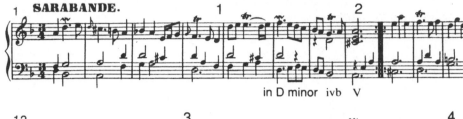

in D minor   ivb   V

Now, to round off this section, listen to the Sarabande complete.

 LISTEN NOW TO ITEM 26.

6   WRITING

6.1   HARMONIZING A TUNE FROM TCHAIKOVSKY

 VIDEO NOTES
UNIT 16, VIDEO SECTION 1

Introduction

We now come to the last of our three basic skills – writing notes on paper. To revise this, we shall be adding a bass line and harmonies to the tune that comes at the beginning of Tchaikovsky's *Serenade for Strings*.

The point of this video section is for you to see how you can build up the bass line (with attendant harmonies) more or less note by note. You will get more

Figure 2   Piotr Ilyich Tchaikovsky, wearing the robes of the honorary Doctor of Music that he was awarded by Cambridge University in 1893, a few months before his death.

out of the exercise, therefore, if you *don't look ahead* to the 'answers' in the examples below; instead, wait until you reach the appropriate points in the video.

During the video

When you are first asked to stop the video you should play Video Example 1.

Video Example 1

The second time you are asked to stop the video, you should think about which chord progression fits with a melody descending from the tonic to the dominant (see Unit 12, Section 7.3). Specifically, look at the three possible chords shown under the note B in bar 1 of Video Example 2, and decide which works best.

Video Example 2

The third time you are asked to stop the video, ask yourself how you can smooth out the zigzag effect indicated by the arrow in Video Example 3, and avoid repeating the F.

Video Example 3

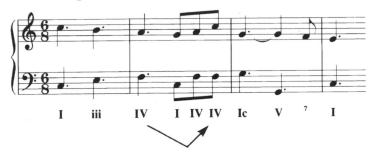

The fourth time that you stop the video, play Video Example 4.

Video Example 4

Summary

Video Example 5 gives the chords we have available for our harmonization of Tchaikovsky's melody.

Video Example 5

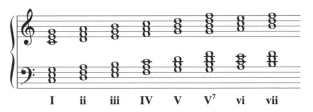

Here are four main points that our harmonization of Tchaikovsky's melody has highlighted. When you proceed to harmonize further melodies during the second half of the course, bear these points in mind.

1　Where possible, use the Ic–V⁷–I cadential progression. Here the melody-pattern under which it fitted was soh-fah-me (see Video Example 6). But it can also be used to harmonize (i) me-ray-doh and (ii) doh-te-doh at the cadence.

Video Example 6

2　Remember that as you approach a perfect cadence, you should not include dominant harmony too close to the cadence. This weakens the effect of the dominant chord at the cadence.

3　Where the melody descends by step from the tonic to the dominant, the chordal progression I–iii–IV–I or I–iii–IV–V is possible, and moreover this is one of the best opportunities for including chord iii. See Video Example 7.

Video Example 7

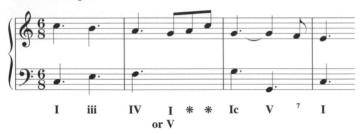

<pre>
I   iii   IV   I   * *   Ic   V   7   I
                        or V
</pre>

4 And, finally, do not forget to consider including first-inversion chords when (i) you have a jagged bass line and (ii) you have the same harmony occurring twice.

---

7 CONCLUSIONS

Since the purpose of this unit has been to help you assess your progress in the course so far, I shall leave you to draw your own conclusions! Admittedly we haven't covered every skill taught in the first half of the course, but we have looked at a representative cross-section. From your success-rate at coping with this, you can judge where you need to spend more time revising.

Don't be too hard on yourself. To proceed with confidence to the rest of the course, you need a good grasp of the essential skills, not a god-like knowledge of absolutely every detail. And don't forget to feel justifiably pleased and encouraged as you tick off those skills you have mastered. But if there are any areas where you feel some improvement would be beneficial, then tackle those now. In this course, a stitch in time definitely saves nine!

8 ANSWERS TO EXERCISES

Exercise 1

Example 39

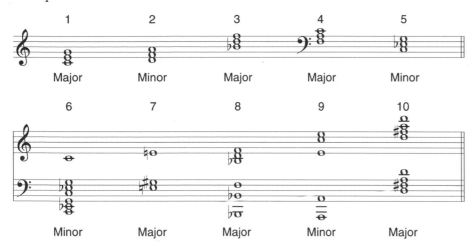

Exercise 2

1 Major	5 Minor
2 Minor	6 Major
3 Major	7 Minor
4 Major	8 Minor

Exercise 3

1 Octave	5 Second
2 Third	6 Second and sixth
3 Sixth	7 Third and sixth
4 Fifth	

Exercise 4

1 Figure

2 Theme

3 Theme

4 Motif

5 Figure

Exercise 5

Example 40

Exercise 6

Example 41   Beethoven, Symphony No. 7, second movement

Example 42   Schubert, Rosamunde, entr'acte

Example 43   Verdi, Rigoletto, 'La donna è mobile'

(Verdi actually notates his melody in ⅜.)

Example 44   *Mozart,* Eine kleine Nachtmusik, *first movement*

or you may well have notated it without the rests, like this:

Example 45   *Holst,* The Planets, *'Jupiter'*

Example 46   *J. Strauss (ii),* Die Fledermaus

Exercise 7

1   Interrupted

2   Perfect

3   Perfect

4   Perfect

Exercise 8

1   Perfect

2   Imperfect

3   Perfect

4   Perfect

ACKNOWLEDGEMENTS

Grateful acknowledgement is made to the following for permission to reproduce material in this unit:

Example 5 (extract from Haydn's String Quartet, Op. 1 No. 1), reproduced by permission of Ernst Eulenberg Ltd.

Figure 1 (Ralph Vaughan Williams), reproduced by courtesy of the National Portrait Gallery.

Figure 2 (Piotr Ilyich Tchaikovsky), Novosti Press Agency.

A214 UNDERSTANDING MUSIC: ELEMENTS, TECHNIQUES AND STYLES

Unit 1	Introducing rhythm	Unit 17	Harmonizing a melody I
Unit 2	More about rhythm; Introducing pitch	Unit 18	Modulation II
		Unit 19	Harmonizing a melody II
Unit 3	Starting with staff notation		
Unit 4	Melody	Unit 20	Following an orchestral score
Unit 5	Harmony I: The chord	Unit 21	Transpositions and reductions
Unit 6	Modes, scales and keys		
		Unit 22	Formal principles II
Unit 7	Primary triads	Unit 23	Baroque style study I
Unit 8	Cadences	Unit 24	Classical style study I
Unit 9	Following a score I	Unit 25	Some points of style
Unit 10	Formal principles I	Unit 26	Baroque style study II
		Unit 27	Classical style study II
Unit 11	First inversion chords		
Unit 12	Secondary diatonic triads (II, III, VI and VII)	Unit 28	The Romantic period
Unit 13	Modulation I	Unit 29	Style, history and canon
Unit 14	Following a score II	Unit 30	Baroque style study III
Unit 15	Two-stave reduction	Unit 31	Classical style study III
Unit 16	Mostly revision	Unit 32	Towards the examination: Writing about music